*NOTES ON PROSODY*

and

*ABRAM GANNIBAL*

*Vladimir Nabokov*

# NOTES ON PROSODY

## and

# ABRAM GANNIBAL

From the Commentary to the author's
translation of Pushkin's EUGENE ONEGIN

BOLLINGEN SERIES

PRINCETON UNIVERSITY PRESS

# Contents

---

NOTES ON PROSODY

Author's Note     vii

1. Prosodies     3
2. Feet     4
3. The Scud     9
4. Tilted Scuds     17
5. Spondees     27
6. Elisions     30
7. The Origination of Metrical Verse in Russia     33
8. Difference in Modulation     46
9. Examples of Modulations     51
10. Counts of Modulations in *Eugene Onegin*     69
11. Other Meters and Rhythms     76
12. Differences in Use of Meter     80
13. Rhyme     82
Index     97

ABRAM GANNIBAL

Foreword     107
Pushkin's Comments Published During
His Lifetime     108

# Contents

Pushkin's Ancestors     111

The Documents     112

Dates of Abram Gannibal's Birth and Death     114

Gannibal's Origin     116

Gannibal's Birthplace     118

Gannibal's Sister     125

Gannibal's Parentage     127

Gannibal's Enslavement     131

Gannibal in Turkey     134

Gannibal and Raguzinski     139

Gannibal's First Years in Russia (1706–16)     143

Gannibal in Western Europe (1716–23)     148

Gannibal and Annibal     152

Gannibal's Later Years in Russia (1723–81)     153

Conclusions     155

Works Consulted     162

Index     169

## AUTHOR'S NOTE

The following Notes on Prosody represent part (Appendix Two) of my Commentary to Aleksandr Pushkin's novel in verse, *Eugene Onegin*. The work, containing this commentary, with two appendixes, index, my critical translation of the novel, and a reproduction of the original 1837 edition, was published in four volumes in Bollingen Series, New York, and by Routledge and Kegan Paul, London.

A few corrections, chiefly typographical, have been made for this reprinting. There was not space for a footnote that I should have liked to add, on p. 47, asterisked to the phrase "monosyllabic adjectives" in line 4 of paragraph 2, to wit: "Not counting, of course, the monosyllabic predicative forms—adverbish mongrels, really—of disyllabic adjectives, such as *glup*, 'is stupid,' from *glupïy*, or *bel*, 'is white,' from *belïy*."

*

The sketch of Abram Gannibal's life constitutes Appendix One of my Commentary to *Eugene Onegin*. Previous to its appearance in the four-volume edition, it was published in a somewhat abridged form, entitled "Pushkin and Gannibal," in *Encounter* (London), XIX: 3 (September 1962).

V. N.

*NOTES ON PROSODY*

*Notes on Prosody*

---

The following notes on English and Russian iambic tetrameters are intended only to outline the differences and
similarities between them. Pushkin is taken as the greatest representative of Russian poetry; the differences
between his iambic tetrameters and those of other masters of the meter among minor and major Russian poets
are matters of specific, not generic, distinction. Russian
prosody, which came into existence only two centuries
ago, is tolerably well known to native students: some
good work has been done by a number of Russian theorists in relation to *Eugene Onegin*. On the other hand, the
huge and ancient English genus is very imperfectly
described. I have not been particularly interested in the
question, but as much as I can recall I have not come
across a single work that treated English iambics —
particularly the tetrameter—on a taxonomical and
comparative-literature basis, in a way even remotely acceptable to a student of prosody. In my casual perusals,

*3*

I have of course slammed shut without further ado any such works on English prosody in which I glimpsed a crop of musical notes or those ridiculous examples of strophic arrangements which have nothing to do with the structure of verse. In other works, muddleheaded discussions of "short" and "long," "quantity" and "equivalence," not only contain various traditional nonsense or subjective illusions of sense but do not afford any systematic notion of the iambic modulation beyond tedious arguments around and around "apostrophization," "substitution," "spondees," and so forth. In consequence, I have been forced to invent a simple little terminology of my own, explain its application to English verse forms, and indulge in certain rather copious details of classification before even tackling the limited object of these notes to my translation of Pushkin's *Eugene Onegin*, an object that boils down to very little— in comparison to the forced preliminaries—namely, to a few things that the non-Russian student of Russian literature must know in regard to Russian prosody in general and to *Eugene Onegin* in particular.

## 2. FEET

If by prosodies we mean systems or forms of versification evolved in Europe during this millennium and used by her finest poets, we can distinguish two main species, the syllabic system and the metrical one, and a subspecific form belonging to the second species (but not inconsistent with certain syllabic compositions), cadential poetry, in which all that matters is lilt depending on random numbers of accents placed at random intervals. A fourth form, which is specifically vague and is rather a catchall than a definite category (not yet having been instrumental in producing great poetry), takes care of unrhymed free verse, which, except for the presence of typographical turnpikes, grades insensibly into prose, from a taxonomic point of view.

Except in one or two special cases, Greek and Latin verse forms are not taken into consideration in the following notes, and such terms as "iambic tetrameter" and so forth are not meant to suggest their ancient application, whatever that was, but are used strictly in reference to modern types of prosody, as convenient and innocuous nomenclatorial handles, instead of such ambiguous terms, in relation to metrical verse, as "octosyllables," and so forth. A foot is not only the basic element of meter but, in action, becomes the meter itself: a "monometer" is a line of one foot, and so on, to "hexameter," a six-foot line, beyond which the metrical line is no longer felt as a line and breaks into two.

Taken all in all, and with our quest limited to the latter half of the millennium in question, the greatest representative of the syllabic prosody in delicacy and complexity of modulation is certainly the French Alexandrine. The student is generally taught that its three characteristics are: an obligatory equality of syllables (twelve in masculine lines, thirteen in feminine ones), obligatory rhyme (in couplets or in any other arrangement, but with no two different masculine or feminine endings occurring in adjacent lines), and an obligatory caesura after the sixth syllable, which must be accented (or, if this is followed by a final *e muet*, the latter must be neutralized by an apocopate fusion with the vowel heading the second hemistich). Apart from niceties of instrumentation, which, after all, can be paralleled in other prosodies, but to which the French ear seems to be especially sensitive, a major part in the composition of the Alexandrine is played by a combination of the following elements (of which the first is, of course, a feature of other syllabic lengths as well). It should always be remembered that, whatever prosody is followed, the art of the poet depends on certain contrasts and concords, constraints and liberties, denials and yieldings:

(1) The *e muet*: the interplay between the theoretical or generic value of the unelided *e muet* (which is never heard as a full semeion, as all the other vowels in the line are) and its actual or specific value in a given line. The number of such incomplete semeia and their distribution allow endless variations of melody, in conjunction with the neutralizing effect of apocopes in any part of the line. There are two main varieties of *e muet*, especially noticeable in rhymes (see §13, Rhyme).

(2) The interplay between the prosodically existing pause in mid-line and another pause, or pauses, or absence of pause, proceeding from the inward rhythm or logical sense, or irrational lilt, of the line. Especially beautiful effects have been achieved by the so-called romantics after the pedestrian eighteenth century had all but stamped out French poetry. This kind of acrobatic shifting back and forth across the constant caesural ha-ha is something not duplicated in English or Russian iambic pentameters (of the blank-verse type), in which the artificial caesural pause after the second foot is triumphantly sung out of metrical existence by a Milton or a Pushkin. In the French Alexandrine the caesura is well adjusted to the rhythm of human breath in slow reading, while, on the other hand, secondary pauses owing to "shifts" allow for precipitated or delayed exhalations.

(3) The enjambment or run-on, a fertile source of modulation, which is too well known from its presence in English iambics to need any explication here.

(4) The rich rhyme (which is especially beautiful *when* enjambed, just as the caesural pause is especially enhanced *when* sense glides across it). It is imitated by the Russian rule of rhyme, which will be discussed later.

The metrical system, on the other hand, is based first

of all on a regular recurrence of rhythm within a line of verse, in which foot stress tends to coincide with accent (word stress), and nonstress with nonaccent. This recurrence is seen as a sequence of similar feet. Each such foot can consist of either two or three divisions (semeia), one of which is stressed by the meter but not necessarily by the syllable of the word coinciding with it. This stressed division is called the ictus, while the unstressed divisions are called depressions. Mathematically, only five kinds of feet can exist: the iamb, the trochee, the anapaest, the amphibrach, and the dactyl.

For the final foot to be complete, the presence of one semeion is sufficient, provided it is an ictus. Conversely, the identity of the meter is not affected by any number of unstressed syllables coming after the final ictus of the line. This final ictus and these additions to it are called "terminals." A line terminating in an ictus is called "masculine"; a line terminating in one unstressed syllable is called "feminine." If the terminals of two, not necessarily adjacent, lines correspond in sound, the result is a "rhyme." The rhyme is masculine if the ultima of the last word of the line is stressed and coincides with the ictus. It is feminine if the penultimate coincides with the ictus, and "synthetic" or "long" if it is the antepenultimate that is stressed.

The samples given below illustrate the five combinations (of one ictus and one or two depressions) mathematically possible within the limits of one metrical foot. The first two are masculine tetrameters: (1) iambic and (2) trochaic; the rest are masculine trimeters: (3) dactylic, (4) amphibrachic, and (5) anapaestic.

      (1) The rós- | es áre | agaín | in blóom
      (2) Róses | áre a- | gáin in | blóom
      (3) Róses a- | gáin are in | blóom
      (4) The róses | agaín are | in blóom
      (5) And the rós- | es agaín | are in blóom

An example of pausative or cadential verse using the same words would run:

And again the rose is in bloom

which the metrically trained ear hears as three anapaests with one missed depression in the second foot causing a little gasp or pause, hence the term.

And a syllabic line would be:

De nouveau la rose fleurit

in which the *e* of *rose* is a type of depression that cannot be rendered in English, German, or Russian.

An iambic foot cannot be illustrated by a word unless that word is part of a specific iambic line. An iambic foot can be illustrated by signs only insofar as these signs are made to express the maximal four variations in which an iambic foot actually appears in verse:

$\cup \; \perp$   regular beat
$\cup \; -$   scud (or false pyrrhic)
$\cup̓ \; -$   tilted scud (or false trochee)
$\cup̓ \; \perp$   false spondee

To the discussion of these we shall now turn.

An ordinary iambic foot (i.e., one not affected by certain contractional and rhymal variations) consists of two semeia, the first semeion being called a depression ($\cup$ or $\cup̓$) and the second an ictus ($-$ or $\perp$). Any such foot belongs to one of the following types (with the basic metrical stress marked $-$, and the variable word accent $'$):

(1) Regular foot, $\cup\!\perp$ (unaccented nonstress followed by accented stress); e.g., "Appéase my grief, and déadly páin" (Earl of Surrey, *The Lover Describeth His Restless State*).

(2) Scudded foot (or false pyrrhic), $\cup -$ (unaccented nonstress followed by unaccented stress); e.g., "In expec-

tátion of a guést" (Tennyson, *In Memoriam*, VI) and "In lóveliness of pérfect déeds" (ibid., XXXVI).

(3) Tilt (or inversion), ⌣ – (accented nonstress followed by unaccented stress); e.g., "Sense of intólerable wróng" (Coleridge, *The Pains of Sleep*), "Vaster than Émpires and more slów" (Marvell, *To His Coy Mistress*), and "Perfectly púre and góod: I fóund" (Browning, *Porphyria's Lover*).

(4) False spondee, ⌣ ⊥ (accented nonstress and accented stress); e.g., "Twice hóly wás the Sábbath-béll" (Keats, *The Eve of St. Mark*).

## 3. THE SCUD

We speak of an "accent" in relation to a word and of a "stress" in relation to a metrical foot. A "scud" is an unaccented stress. "An inextínguishable fláme" has two accented and two unaccented stresses.

When in verse a weak monosyllabic word (i.e., one not accented in speech) or a weak syllable of a long word happens to coincide with the stressed part (ictus) of a foot, there results a modulation that I term a "scud."

If an accented syllable in speech be notated ′, and a stress accent in verse ⊥, then a scud is marked –.

The unstressed part of a foot is marked ⌣ (for which a "depression" is the best term).*

The verse quoted above is notated: ⌣ – ⌣ ⊥ ⌣ – ⌣ ⊥.

A scud can occur in any foot of any metrical line but is far more frequent in double-semeion meters or "binaries" (iambs and trochees) than in triple-semeion meters or "ternaries" (anapaests, amphibrachs, and

---

*When in verse a strong monosyllable coincides with a depression, the resulting element is marked ⌣, but the use of this sign is really necessary only in the case of "tilts" (of which further).

dactyls).* We shall be mainly concerned with scuds in the iambic tetrameter.

Weak—i.e., scuddable—monosyllables may be described as follows:

Monosyllables that are of comparatively minor importance (articles, prepositions, etc.), unless especially emphasized, and that are not usually rhymed on, are counted as scuds equivalent to unaccented but metrically stressed syllables in longer words (actually, this is truer of English than Russian, because in Russian verse a scud provided by a monosyllable is a trifle less fluid than one provided by a polysyllable—which, of course, has no secondary accent in Russian). Between a typical weak monosyllable (such as "the") and an indubitably accented one (such as querulous "why"), there are gradations and borderline cases ("while," "when," "had," etc.), which may be termed "semiscuds." To determine them depends so much upon context, and is often so subjective a matter—in reference to random lines, at least—that one is not inclined to furnish a special mark for them (say, ⌣). I have disregarded them in my percentile calculations. Semiscuds are not frequent enough in either English or Russian to affect numerical results when dealing with relatively small samples (say, fifty lines per poet). A special study of scuds, however, should take into account the fact that if we examine such Russian or English dipodies as:

*eyo toski*, which means, and is accented, "of her distress"
*i on ubit*, which means, and is accented, "and he is killed"

we cannot but notice that if these syllables are iambized, the first ictus in each case is somewhat less strongly emphasized than in:

---

*A good example of scuds in the amphibrachic trimeter is Praed's *Good-Night to the Season*, ll. 23–4:
    "Misrepresentations of reasons
    And misunderstandings of notes."

*nemoy toski*, which means, and is accented, "of mute distress"

*i Dzhim ubit*, which means, and is accented, "and Jim is killed."

Among indubitably scudded monosyllables the most obvious ones are: "a," "an," "and," "as," "at," "but," "for," "from," "if," "in," "like," "of," "on," "or," "the," "to," etc.

The scudding of such particles as "all," "no," "not," "was," etc., is a question of context and individual taste.

Similarly, in Russian, obvious and unquestionable scuds are: *dlya* ("for"), *do* ("till"), *i* ("and"), *na* ("on"), *ne* ("not," a word that should never be accented in good Russian), *no* ("but"), *ot* ("from"), *po* ("along"), *pod* ("under"), *u* ("at"), etc., whereas the scudding of *bïl* ("was"), *net* ("no"), etc., depends on context and elective intonation.

When we turn to polysyllabics, the first thing we notice is an important accentual difference between English and Russian, and this has a definite repercussion on the frequency of pure scuds. In Russian, a polysyllabic word, no matter how long (provided it is not a blatantly artificial compound with the seam showing), can bear but one accent, and consequently a word of any length can bear only one stress accent in verse. Neither *neveroyátneyshie* ("most improbable," pl.) nor *vïkarab-kavshiesya* ("scrambled out," pl.) has more than one accent. The first can easily be woven into a mellifluous iambic tetrameter (in which the last word means "dreams"):

*neveroyátneyshie snï*

whereas the shortest measure into which the second may be crammed is a somewhat bumpy trochaic pentameter:

*vïkarabkavshiesya kott*

(which means, in prose, "the cats that have scrambled out").

In English polysyllabic words, on the other hand, there may occur a secondary accent, especially in American speech, but still there are numerous long words that have only one accent, such as "guárdedly" or "considering." The secondary accent is found, for example, on the third syllable of the following word, when pronounced the American way: "mátrimòny"; but in British parlance, and thus in poetry written by Englishmen, it should be scanned "mátrimony." In the various examples of verses given further I shall disregard secondary accents when not intended by an English author, but the fact remains that a number of ordinary compounds, constantly recurring in poetry, do bear the ghost of an additional accent, with a resulting semiscud, such as "òvermúch" or "sèmidiámeters," whereas their Russian counterparts, *chereschúr* and *poludiámetrï*, are strictly single-accented.

In regard to nomenclature, I should note at this point that Russian theorists use or have used for, or in connection with, the element I call a scud the terms *pirríhiy* ("pyrrhic"), *peon* ("paeon"), *poluudarenie* ("half stress" or "half accent"), and *uskorenie* ("acceleration"). None is satisfactory. The notation of the pyrrhic ($\cup \cup$) suits, at best, two adjacent depressions in a line of ternaries, since it suggests an identical absence of stress and accent on both syllables, whereas the point is, of course, that there persists the shadow of the expected metrical beat on one of the semeia of a binary foot when it is scudded (nor can the pyrrhic be used in the sense of a foot in speaking of scuds in anapaests, amphibrachs, and dactyls, in which it is, as just said, a basic component). The same considerations apply to the paeon, which is a bulky thing containing two binaries ($\cup \perp \cup \cup$ or $\cup \cup \cup \perp$, and there are other variations), so that the verse "the inextinguishable flame" would be represented by two paeons of the type ∪∪∪´, whereas the verse "extinguishable is the flame" would be represented by both types. If the "paeon" is too big for use, the "half stress" or "half accent" is too small, since it strictly limits to one semeion the idea of "scud" (which, although focused on one semeion, affects the whole foot, especially in "tilt" variations). Moreover, this would entail terming the incomplete scud a "three-quarter accent," which would lead to cumbersome complications. Finally, the term "acceleration" is misleading because second-foot scuds have an exactly opposite—namely, slowing-down —effect upon the line.

In English theories of prosody scuds have been described as "weak places," which is too vague and ambiguous for recurrent nomenclatorial use, and defined as "omitted stresses," which is meaningless, since the metrical stress of a scudded foot is not "omitted," but merely not trodden upon by the unaccented syllable of the passing word, which, however, is aware of the unused steppingstone it skims.

The scudding of iambic tetrameters produces, in English, four simple varieties (of which, as we shall presently see, variety IV can hardly be said to be represented in Russian poetry); the scudded feet are underlined in the following examples:

I  ∪ − ∪ ´ ∪ ´ ∪ ´  Thĕ dīsregarded thing we break
                    Ĭs ōf the kind we cannot make;

II  ∪ ´ ∪ − ∪ ´ ∪ ´  We break thĕ dīsregarded thing,
                    Not thinkĭng ōf its wistful ring;

III  ∪ ´ ∪ ´ ∪ − ∪ ´  We break the thing wĕ dīsregard,
                    We break the statŭe ōf a bard

IV  ∪ ´ ∪ ´ ∪ ´ ∪ −  Near which an age was lingĕr-
                    īng;

o ◡ ⌐ ◡ ⌐ ◡ ⌐ ◡ ⌐ We take the thing and break the thing.

(The last example is, of course, a scudless line.)

The following are examples of combinations of the above scuds:

I + II + IV ◡ – ◡ – ◡ ⌐ ◡ – Ĭncōmprĕhēnsibilĭtȳ,

I + III ◡ – ◡ ⌐ ◡ – ◡ ⌐ Thĭs īn the unĭvērse we see;

I + II ◡ – ◡ – ◡ ⌐ ◡ ⌐ Ănd, īn thĕ cōnflagration blent,

I + IV ◡ – ◡ ⌐ ◡ ⌐ ◡ – Stărs ānd the awful firmămēnt

II + IV ◡ ⌐ ◡ – ◡ ⌐ ◡ – Shine distăntlȳ and silĕntlȳ

II + III ◡ ⌐ ◡ – ◡ – ◡ ⌐ On wildĕrnēssĕs ānd on me.

Of the above six forms, only I + III (not too frequent in English, but fairly frequent in Russian) and II + III (about as infrequent in Russian as in English) have Russian counterparts.

Other possibilities are, theoretically, III + IV, I + II + III, I + III + IV, but they are artificial tongue-twisters of no prosodical importance. I have omitted the accent on "stars" (◡̆) for simplicity's sake; the foot is a tilt-scudded one (◡̆ –) instead of the basic ◡ ⌐. (See § 4, Tilted Scuds.)

The scuds in the same verse and those in adjacent verses, when connected with lines, may form various figures, which express the modulation of the piece. Andrey Belïy (1880–1934), the inventor of this diagrammatic system, was the first to reveal that certain frequences of scuds (which he called *poluudareniya*, "half stresses") and certain geometrical figures resulting from their being connected by lines (triangles, quadrangles, trapezoids, etc.) were characteristic of this or that Russian poet's iambic tetrameters.* When I was still a boy, I was greatly fascinated by Belïy's admirable work, but have not consulted it since I last read it in 1919.

---

*See his tables, "Opït harakteristiki russkogo chetïryohstopnogo yamba," in *Simvolizm*, a collection of essays (Moscow, 1910).

If we apply the Belian system to the fourteen lines, above, given as examples of scudding, but use a slightly different kind of notation (with scudded feet represented by x's and scudless feet by o's), we obtain the following scheme:

| I | II | III | IV |
|---|----|-----|----|
| x | o | o | o |
| x | o | o | o |
| o | x | o | o |
| o | x | o | o |
| o | o | x | o |
| o | o | x | o |
| o | o | o | x |
| o | o | o | o |
| x | x | o | x |
| x | o | x | o |
| x | x | o | o |
| x | o | o | x |
| o | x | o | x |
| o | x | x | o |

For the sake of easy reference I have collected, below, some English examples of scud modulation. They are mostly culled from Tennyson's *In Memoriam* (1850), which is by far his best work, and are then marked by the numeral of their section. The rest are added because not found in *In Memoriam*. Scudded feet are underlined.

      *Scudless:* ∪ ∠ ∪ ∠ ∪ ∠ ∪ ∠

| | |
|---|---|
| Defécts of dóubt, and taínts of blóod | [LIV] |
| And "Áve, Áve, Áve," saíd | [LVII] |
| The líttle víllage lóoks forlórn | [LX] |

      *Scud* I: ∪ – ∪ ∠ ∪ ∠ ∪ ∠

| | |
|---|---|
| And with the thoúght her cólour búrns | [VI] |
| The generátions eách with eách | [XL] |
| Imaginátions cálm and faír | [XCIV] |

      *Scud* II: ∪ ∠ ∪ – ∪ ∠ ∪ ∠

| | |
|---|---|
| In lóveliness of pérfect déeds | [XXXVI] |

*15*

And thíne in undiscóver'd lánds     [xl]
A frésh associátion blów     [ci]

*Scud* iii: ∪ ́ ∪ ∪ ́ ∪ − ∪ ́
The fár-off ínterest of teárs     [i]
She tákes a ríband or a róse     [vi]
In vaín; a fávourable speéd     [ix]

*Scud* iv: ∪ ́ ∪ ∪ ́ ∪ ́ ∪ −
The práise that cómes to cónstancy     [xxi]
Defámed by évery chárlatan     [cxi]

*Scuds* i+ii: ∪ − ∪ − ∪ ́ ∪ ́
As on The Lariáno crépt
        [Tennyson, *The Daisy*]

*Scuds* i+iii: ∪ − ∪ ́ ∪ − ∪ ́
In expectátion of a guést     [vi]
My capabílities of lóve     [lxxxv]
A contradíction on the tóngue     [cxxv]
On the bald stréet breaks the blank dáy     [vii]
[Cf.] To a green Thoúght in a green Sháde   [Marvell,
        *The Garden*]

*Scuds* i+iv: ∪ − ∪ ́ ∪ ́ ∪ −
All-comprehénsive ténderness,     [lxxxv]
All-subtilísing íntellect

*Scuds* ii+iv: ∪ ́ ∪ − ∪ ́ ∪ −
On glórious insufficíencies     [cxii]
With ágonies, with énergies     [cxiii]

*Scuds* ii+iii: ∪ ́ ∪ − ∪ − ∪ ́
Most músicall, most melanchóly     [Milton,
        *Il Penseroso*]
This Éxtasie doth unperpléx     [John Donne,
        *The Extasie*]

Below is the analysis of fifty-line-long samples of
scudded and scudless iambic tetrameters from ten com-

positions, of which eight are by English authors. Three belong to the seventeenth century, one to the eighteenth, and four to the nineteenth: Donne's *The Extasie*, ll. 1–50; Butler's *Hudibras*, pt. I, can. I, ll. 187–236; Marvell's *The Nymph Complaining for the Death of Her Fawn*, ll. 73–122; Cowper's *Written after Leaving Her at New Burns*, 49 ll. in all; Coleridge's *The Pains of Sleep*, ll. 1–50; Tennyson's *In Memoriam*, ll. 1–50; Browning's *Porphyria's Lover*, ll. 1–50; and Arnold's *Resignation*, ll. 1–50. These are compared to two sequences of similar length from Lomonosov's *Ode to Empress Elizabeth* (1747), and from Pushkin's *Evgeniy Onegin*, Four : IX–XII : 1–8 (1825). Semiscuds are not counted in any of the samples, and these are not large enough to permit more than a general impression of comparative scud frequency.

| | I | II | III | IV | I-II | I-III | I-IV | II-III | II-IV | O |
|---|---|---|---|---|---|---|---|---|---|---|
| Donne | 6 | 4 | 8 | 2 | 1 | 1 | | 1 | 1 | 26 |
| Butler | 6 | 5 | 8 | 6 | | 3 | | | 1 | 21 |
| Marvell | 16 | 4 | 8 | 1 | | 1 | | | 1 | 19 |
| Cowper | 12 | 4 | 7 | | 1 | | 1 | | | 25 |
| Coleridge | 5 | 8 | 2 | 1 | | 4 | | 1 | | 29 |
| Tennyson | 3 | 1 | 4 | | | | | | | 42 |
| Browning | 6 | 2 | 6 | | | | | | | 36 |
| Arnold | 6 | 10 | 5 | 1 | | 1 | 1 | | | 26 |
| Lomonosov | 1 | 8 | 24 | | | 2 | | 1 | | 14 |
| Pushkin | 3 | 3 | 31 | | | 6 | | | | 7 |

See also § 9, Examples of Modulations.

#### 4. TILTED SCUDS

In reference to an iambic line, a typical or unqualified "tilt" denotes a sequence of accented depression and unaccented stress, ∪́ – (instead of the expected ∪ –́ or ∪ –), coinciding with any foot in the line.* Any tilt is a tilted scud, since the stress in such feet is not accented. English theorists term tilted scuds "inversion of stress"; a better description would be "inversion of accent," since it is the word stress that (more or less gracefully) feigns a surrender to the meter. The meter is basic and cannot succumb to the word.

Typical tilts in English iambics, to which they add considerable beauty, belong to four varieties insofar as number and length of words are involved in their producement:

(1) The frequent "split tilt," which consists of an accented monosyllable (say, "deep") and an unaccented one (say, "in");

(2) The not-very-frequent "short tilt," which consists of an accented monosyllable and the unaccented first syllable of the next polysyllabic word ("dark in-"; see example, below);

(3) The fairly frequent "duplex tilt," which consists of a disyllabic word accented on the first syllable in ordinary speech (say, "guarded"); and

(4) The rare "long tilt," which consists of the first and second syllables of a trisyllabic word, accented on the first syllable in ordinary speech ("terri-"; see example, below).

Examples:

(1) *Deep in* the night on mountains steep,
(2) *Dark, in*accessible and proud,
(3) *Guarded* by dragons, castles sleep;
(4) *Terri*ble stars above them crowd.

---

*Even with the last one, if we regard the famous (perhaps, accidentally fivefold, or, perhaps, meant as a prose interpolation) "Never, never, never, never, never!" in *King Lear* (v, iii, 309) as a masculine line in iambic pentameter, entirely consisting of five tilted scuds and thus representing a maximal disembodiment of meter.

The "reverse tilt," which is less interesting artistically, denotes a combination of unaccented stress and accented depression, $- \smile$, instead of the expected $\perp \smile$ or $- \smile$, and may coincide with any even-place, odd-place segment of the iambic line except the last. The result is a scud tilted in reverse.

Reverse tilts come mainly in one variety, the fairly frequent "split reverse tilt," which consists of two monosyllables, the first unaccented and the second accented:

> Sweet is the shiver *of cold* Spring
> when birds, in garden *and grove*, sing.

There are two reverse tilts here: "of cold" and "and grove"; both are notated $- \smile$; but in the first line the accent (on "cold") is slighter, and metrically more acceptable, than the accent on "grove" in the second line. "Cold" is connected logically with the next word ("spring") and therefore skims on with the impetus of anticipation; it constitutes a common variation throughout the history of English iambics; but the logical beat on "grove" is equivalent in speech to that on the first syllable of "garden," with which it is phrasally linked; in result, the voice strains unduly to combine accent and stress, and the effect is jarring to the ear unless accepted as a deliberate experiment in rhythm variation transcending the meter. It will be noticed, incidentally, that if the second verse is read with a strict adherence to meaning, the prosodical result of "grove, sing" is, in binaries, the closest possible approach to a spondee (two adjacent stress accents); but they are separated by a pause (and it is in pausative variations that we take off from the metrical system in the direction of cadential forms).

Another variety, the "duplex reverse tilt," consisting of a disyllabic word accented on the second syllable

against the grain of a stress-unstress sequence of semeia
(in the even-odd places of an iambic verse or in the odd-
even places of a trochaic one), inevitably produces a
harsh and uncouth effect, since the accent does not sub-
mit to the stress as flexibly as it does in the ordinary
duplex tilt. Metrically, the iambic foot is stronger than
the trochaic word; dictionally, the iambic word is more
self-conscious, and thus stronger, than the trochaic foot.
Reverse tilts have been vaguely designated as "recession
of accent" by English theorists; e.g., Robert Bridges, in
*Milton's Prosody* (Oxford, 1893, pp. 52–61).

As with all modulations in iambic meter, the beauty
of tilt, especially of duplex tilt, which is such an admirable and natural feature of English iambic pentameter,
and gives such allure to the rare lines in which Russian
poets use it, lies in a certain teasing quality of rhythm,
in the tentative emergence of an intonation that *seems*
in total opposition to the dominant meter, but actually
owes its subtle magic to the balance it tends to achieve
between yielding and not yielding—yielding to the meter and still preserving its accentual voice. Only a blunt
ear can perceive in it any "irregularity of meter," and
only an old-fashioned pedant would treat it as the in-
trusion of another species of meter. In English poetry,
its carefree admission by major poets, especially in the
beginning of the iambic lines, is owing partly to the comparative scarcity of such words in English as conform to
the regular iambic foot and partly to accents in English
words not being so strong and exclusive as they are in,
say, Russian.

I use the new term "tilt" or "tilted scud" in prefer-
ence to "nonterminal wrenched accent," because
physically no special wrench is involved; on the contrary, what happens is an elegant sliding movement, the
tipping of a wing, the precise dipping of a balance.
"Hovering accent" is ambiguous; and still more ob-

jectionable is the crude term "trochaic substitution," suggesting as it does a mechanical replacement of one block of elements by another block. The whole point of the device lies precisely in the iambization of a trochaic, or sometimes even dactylic, word. It is not a substitution, but a reconciliation: the graceful submission of a noniambic word to the dominant iambic meter of the verse. Further confusion arises from the fact that tilts can, and do, also occur in trochaic lines (in which case the sequence of places that a duplex tilt, say, occupies is not odd-even, as in an iambic line, but even-odd).

Duplex tilts have nothing to do with certain emancipations of meter that form a gradation toward cadential verse (e.g., the recurrent substitution, in the course of a piece, of one entire foot, in, say, an iambic tetrameter, by a triplex foot represented by a word, or words, that cannot be elided). George Saintsbury, for example, who somehow sees tilts as forms of "equivalence," gets hopelessly muddled in his treatment of these modulations.

The application of "wrenched accent" should be limited to forced terminals; i.e., to an artificial switch of accent, in a disyllabic rhyme word, from feminine ("Éngland") to masculine ("Englánd").

When we turn to an examination of tilts in Russian iambic tetrameters, the following facts transpire:

Split and short tilts are as natural a modulation in Russian as they are in English but occur less frequently. They are definitely rare in *EO*.

The split tilt is even less frequent than the short tilt, whereas the contrary is true in the case of English, where the long word is less frequent in the $1+4$ or $1+5$ or $1+6$ or $1+7$ syllable compartments of the line (where it has to sprawl in order to crowd out, as it were, the lone initial monosyllable of the line and thus produce the short tilt).

Finally (and here we have one of the main differences

between English and Russian prosodies as used by major poets), the duplex tilt, in any part of the line, does not exist in Russian trochaics or iambics (except for the small group of certain two-syllable prepositions, to be discussed further).

The split tilt is represented in *EO* by such more or less widely scattered lines as, for example:

Eight : XVII : 3:   *Kák? iz glushí stepníh seléniy* . . .
               How? from the dépth of prairie
                  hómesteads . . .

Eight : XVII : 11:   *Knyáz' na Onégina glyadít\**. . .
                prínce at Onégin [tum-tee] lóoks . . .

Seven : XVII : 10:   *Kíy na bil'yárde otdïhál* . . .
                cúe on the bílliard did repóse . . .

Six : XL : 13:   *Tám u ruch'yá v tení gustóy* . . .
                thére, by the bróok, in sháde opáque . . .

In this last example the tilt is not so strong as in the preceding ones, and there are in *EO* a certain number of other tiltings of even less strength, such as on *gde* ("where"), *on* ("he"), etc., which are only semitilts.

The short tilt is represented by such lines as:

Three : IX : 4:   *P'yót obol'stítel'nïy obmán* . . .
              drínks irresístible decéit ["imbibes
                the ravishing illusion" would, of
                course, be a closer rendering of the
                contextual sense] . . .

One : XXXIII : 7:   *Nét, nikogdá sred' pílkih dnéy* . . .
                Nó, [tum-]not ónce mid férvid
                dáys . . .

---

\*Here, and elsewhere, the obligatory article and absence of inflective extensions in English make it impossible to render, with any elegance or completeness, both sense and scansion in the same number of semeia. The translation follows the word order.

Six : v : 14:  *V dólg osushát' butílki trí . . .*
       [The meaning is "on credit to drain
       some three bottles."]

Two : XXVIII : 4:  *Zvyózd ischezáet horovód . . .*
       [*Zvyozd*, "of stars," *ischezaet*, "dis-
       appears," *horovod*, a choral round
       dance performed in the open by
       Russian peasant men and maidens.
       The sense is "the choral dance of
       stars is disappearing."]

The duplex tilt does not occur freely in Russian verse: *
its use is strictly limited to a dozen or so humble and
servile disyllables, which, in speech, are accented on
the first syllable but in verse are made, if need be, to
undergo a neutralization of accent by scudding. In Pushkin's poems, these words are: *cherez* ("across," "over"),
*chtobï* ("in order to," "so that," "lest"), *dabï* ("so as
to"), *ili* ("or," "either"), *mezhdu* ("between," "among"),
*oto* (the extended form of *ot*, "from," as used before some
words beginning with certain combinations of consonants such as *vs*), and *pered* ("before," "in front of"):†

*Ruslan and Lyudmíla,*
       I : 22:  *Cherez lesá, cherez moryá . . .*
       Over the woods, over the seas . . .

---

*I notice that on p. 39 of his frankly compilatory *Russian Versi-
fication* (Oxford, 1956), Prof. Boris Unbegaun, when speaking
of the device here termed "tilts," is misled by one of his author-
ities and makes a singular error in his *only* (would-be) example
of a duplex tilt in Russian verse by assuming that the first word
in the iambic line that he quotes from the poem *Fireplace in
Moscow* (*Kamin v Moskve*), published in Penza, 1795, by the
poetaster Prince Ivan Dolgoruki, is pronounced *krásen*, when
actually here it should be *krasyón* (despite the absence of the
diacritical sign)—which, of course, eliminates the "trochaic
substitution."

†Not only *oto*, but each of the other words (except *dabï*), pos-
sesses an abbreviated form: *chtob*, *chrez*, *il'*, *mezh*, *pred*; the
last four are mainly used in verse (cf. "amid" and "mid,"
"over" and "o'er," etc.).

*EO*, Six : XVII : 11:   *Chtobï dvuhútrenniy tsvetók . . .*
        [which means: "lest a two-morn-
        old blossom"]

Six : VII : 2:   *Dabï pozávtrakat' vtroyóm . . .*
        [which means: "so as to lunch
        all three" (*à trois*)]

Seven : II : 9:   *Ili mne chúzhdo naslazhdén'e?*
        [which means: "or is enjoyment
        strange to me"]

Eight : "Onegin's
Letter" : 17:   *Oto vsegó,* \* *chto sérdtsu mílo . . .*
        [which means: "from all that to
        the heart is dear"]

One : LI : 6:   *Pered Onéginïm sobrálsya . . .*
        [which means: "before Onegin
        there assembled"]

Lines beginning with these neutralized words are few in *EO*. It is therefore of great interest to note that in One : LVI, in which our poet affirms his eagerness to differentiate between Onegin and himself, lest the sarcastic reader or some promoter of slander accuse him of narcissism, Pushkin disposes consecutively three lines, each beginning with one of the six tiltable disyllables:

4      *Mezhdu Onéginïm i mnóy,*
         *Chtobï nasméshlivïy chitátel',*
         *Ili kakóy-nibud' izdátel' . . .*
     [the last word meaning "editor,"
"publisher," or "promoter"]

One would almost think that our poet, in 1823, recalled Sumarokov's prosodical experiment of 1759 (see pp. 45–6).

Only one scudded trisyllable occurs in *EO* and in Russian verse generally. This is the staple *peredo* (an end-vowelized form of *pered*, "before," used in speech

---

\*In masculine genitive case endings the gamma of the ultimate is pronounced *v* (*vsevó*).

mainly with *mnoy*, "me," to buffer the clash of consonants), which is normally accented on the first syllable,
but in verse may be tilted in such a way as to coincide
with a depression-beat-depression compartment; e.g., in
*Onegin's Journey*, XVI : 9:

>  *Razóstlan bíl peredo mnóy*

which may be paraphrased so as to render the tilt in the
third foot:

>  befóre me spréad welcoming mé.

Otherwise, the long tilt, rare in English, never occurs in
Russian iambics. An approach to it appears in artificially
compounded epithets, such as this translation of "rosy-
fingered dawn":

>  *Rozovo-pérstnaya zaryá*

in which the hyphen does not prevent the epithet from
becoming a word of six syllables carrying but one accent
on *perst*, despite the fact that in ordinary speech *rozovo*
as a separate adjective or adverb is accented on the first
syllable.

The split reverse tilt occurs now and then in Russian
verse, but on the whole Pushkin avoids it. Curiously
enough, our poet was far from being a lucid theorist in
prosody, but, as in Coleridge's case, the intuition of
genius was a more than sufficient substitute in practice.
In a MS footnote to *EO*, Four : XLI : 7, Pushkin incor-
rectly defends (by notating it as a pyrrhic ⌣⌣ )the jarring
split reverse tilt *vo ves'* ("at all," "in all," "in the
whole"), which as a separate locution is accented in
speech on the *ves'* ("all") and which he scud-tilted in
reverse in two passages:

>  Four : XLI : 7:  *Nesyótsya v góru vo ves' dúh . . .*
>  goes téaring úp hill at all spéed . . .

Three : v : 14:   *I pósle vo ves' pút' molchál . . .*
             and áfter, the whole wáy was múte\* . . .

The duplex reverse tilt is completely banned by Russian major poets (but unintentionally used by some minor ones, such as Vyazemski, Rïleev, and others) because of its association with vulgarity and ineptitude, with the efforts of inexperienced versifiers, as well as with the semiliterate ditties of the servant hall such as the strum songs (*chastushki*) belonging to that deadliest of all folklore, the citified. Thus, in Chapter Four of his admirable novella *The Captain's Daughter* (1833–36), Pushkin, wishing to indicate the poor quality of a madrigal in trochaic tetrameters written by the young "I" of the story, Pyotr Grinyov, has him start l. 7 with a duplex reverse tilt characteristic of such stuff:

> *Oni dúh vo mné smutíli . . .*

*Oni* (sounded as "ah-nee"), which means "they" (referring to Masha Mironov's eyes), is accented on the second syllable in speech but is horribly tilt-scudded in reverse here. The line means "they have confused [*smutili*] the spirit in me." A criticism of this effort, and of the young lady who inspired it, is made by a fellow officer, Aleksey Shvabrin, and leads to an *epée* duel.

The *only* time Pushkin himself, by an unfortunate and incomprehensible oversight, uses a duplex reverse tilt is in l. 21 of his *The Feast at the Time of the Plague* (1830), a blank-verse translation (made from a French prose version) of act I, sc. iv, of *The City of the Plague* (1816), a blank-verse tragedy by John Wilson, alias Christopher North (1785–1854). The trochaically tilted word is *ego* ("his"), which is iambically stressed in speech:

---

\*In the preceding stanza, Three : IV : 2, Pushkin stresses *vo ves'* correctly: . . . *vo ves' opór*, "at full career."

*Ya predlagáyu vĭpit' v ego pámyat'.*
In mémory of hím I suggest drínking.*

Pushkin must have got hold of a fairly accurate version, perhaps with the English original *en regard*.

### 5. SPONDEES

Strictly speaking, the spondee—i.e., two adjacent semeia bearing exactly the same stress accent ($\perp \perp$) and following each other without any break or pause (as might suggest to the ear an inner caesura or missed beat)—is an impossibility in metrical verse as distinguished from cadential or pausative forms. But a kind of false spondee ($\smile \perp$ or $\perp \smile$) is not infrequent.

It should be noted that there are certain disyllabic words, implicitly or actually hyphenated, that in a certain type of speech or under certain emotional conditions can sound like spondees. I have heard Berliners pronounce *Papa* as "pá-pá." American youngsters, especially when stylized on the stage, give the two parts of "gée-whíz" practically the same value. And in slow, deliberate, ruminant American speech, especially in business pronouncements or didactic monologues, such a word as "contact" may become "cón-táct." Any number of other two-syllable formulas of a similar kind can be listed. But the matter is rather of duration and jaw action than of accent, and whenever such a word is used in metrical verse it is bound to become a trochee or an iamb, or a scud, or a tilt; but it never becomes a spondee, unless its hyphen snaps and is replaced by a pause.

> "Good God!" Blanche uttered slowly: "Good
>  God! Look!" I looked, and understood.
> "Rise! Rise!" I loudly cried to her
> "O rise! Rise!" But she did not stir.

---

*Incidentally, Wilson's original (l. 20) reads:
    "Therefore let us drink unto his memory."

If these lines are to scan at all, their only logical rhythm
is:

$$\cup\;\acute{-}\;\cup\;\acute{-}\;\cup\;\acute{-}\;\cup\;\acute{-}$$
$$\cup\;\acute{-}\;\cup\;\acute{-}\;\cup\;-\;\cup\;\acute{-}$$
$$\cup\;\acute{-}\;\cup\;\acute{-}\;\cup\;\acute{-}\;\cup\;\acute{-}$$
$$\cup\;\acute{-}\;\cup\;-\;\cup\;\acute{-}\;\cup\;\acute{-}$$

The force of the meter sorts out the monosyllables in a
certain, iambic, way, and it would be sheer lunacy on a
theorist's part to see "Good God" and "Rise! Rise!" as
spondees. Thus the first "Rise! Rise!" is a rapid attack on
a natural iambic scale, whereas the second set sounds
much more slowly, with the last "Rise" lingering on in
despair. In whatever way they are pronounced, they
belong to the meter.

If we regard the so-called "elegiac pentameter"
(really a dactylic hexameter with the depressions of two
feet, third and sixth, missing) as one line:

$$\acute{-}\quad\cup\cup\quad\acute{-}\quad\cup\quad\cup\acute{-}\quad\acute{-}\quad\cup\cup\quad\acute{-}\quad\cup\cup\quad\acute{-}$$
Cynthia, prim and polite, Cynthia, hard to outwit

then the midway combination of "-lite" and "Cynth-"
may be regarded as a spondee, but a spondee interrupted
by the caesura. This is tantamount to considering the
two hemistichs as two separate verses, each a dactylic
trimeter with a masculine ending. In result, what we
call here a spondee is merely the combined effect of a
strong termination and a strong beginning.

A similar case may crop up in trochees:

Pity, if you have a heart, pretty Nancy Brown,
Who on winter mornings, poor girl, must walk to town.

The second line is unscannable metrically unless we
spade the spondee in two and write or hear these verses
as:

Pity, if you have a heart,
Pretty Nancy Brown,

> Who on winter mornings, poor
> Girl, must walk to town.

The first verse of a famous, though not very good, poem by Tennyson (1842):

> Break, break, break,

if given to read to a person who does not know the entire piece, will probably be scanned as a trio of solid and slow beats devoid of any pathetic sense. For all we know, it might be a boxing referee talking in his sleep. When, however, the dominant rhythm of the poem is known beforehand, then its ternary lilt, broken by pauses, affects by anticipation the scansion of the first line, which may be then scanned either as an anapaestic monometer or, more artistically, as an anapaestic trimeter, with the depressions missing and replaced by rhythmic pauses.

For true spondees, we have to go not to metrical verse but to cadential ones, in which the tonic scansion of what are "irregularities" to the confirmed metrist is of little or no interest:

> Gone is Livia, love is gone:
> Strong wing, soft breast, bluish plume;
> In the juniper tree moaning at dawn:
>     Doom, doom.

It should be noted that in metrical verse the false spondee, when represented by a hyphenated word or by two strong monosyllables, will disclose its metrical leaning as soon as placed in any compartment of an iambic or a trochaic line and should not be confused with disyllables that may be accented either fore or aft. A false spondee will *generally* lean toward the iambic, for the simple reason that, while its first syllable can take care of itself, the second syllable or monosyllable must be especially strongly stress-accented in order to keep up with its predecessor and show what it can do in its turn (this is especially clear when two strong monosyllables coming one after the other are identical words).

In Russian poems false spondees are less frequent than in English ones, only because strong monosyllables are less frequent. Turning to *EO*, we find therein a number of these combinations behaving as English false spondees do. Thus *hleb-sol'* ("bread-salt," meaning "hospitality," "welcome," "shared repast," "good cheer") is metrically duplicated by the sounds of "prep school" or "ebb-sole" (presumably a kind of fish), and *gde, gde* or *tam, tam* by "where, where" and "there, there" respectively. They *may* be placed in a trochaic medium, but (their inclination being iambic) a split reverse tilt will be the only result.

False spondees occur here and there throughout *EO*, but their presence adds little to variety in modulation. In such lines as:

Five : XVII : 7:  *Láy, hóhot, pén'e, svíst i hlóp . . .*
              Barks, laughter, singing, whistling,
               claps . . .

Six : XXXIX : 11:  *Píl, él, skuchál, tolstél, hirél . . .*
              drank, ate, was dull, grew fat,
              decayed . . .

the accents (*Lay*, *Pil*) starting the lines are swept off their respective feet by the strong current of the iambic meter.

## 6. ELISIONS

There are two varieties of elision in English prosody, and it is especially the second that enhances richness of rhythm (the presence or absence of an apostrophe is, of course, merely a typographical detail of no metrical significance; but for the linguist its omission in print sometimes throws light on matters of local or periodic pronunciation).

Of these two varieties the first is the rudimentary apocopation—i.e., the dropping or slurring of a final vowel before an initial vowel in the next word. A standard English apocope is the metrically suggested reading of "many a" as $\overset{\_}{\cup}$ (instead of $\overset{\_}{\cup}\cup$). I find it as early as c. 1393, in John Gower's *Confessio amantis* (bk. III, l. 605). An especially common apocope is the one involving the definite article in such combinations as "th'advice," "th'enemy," and so forth. It is still used in modern metrical verse, but the diacritical sign is dropped, perhaps because of its association with obsolete and artificial forms of poetry.

The second variety of elision is the contraction that implies the elimination from the metrical count of a vowel in the middle of a word. Common contractions are, for example, words that have *ve* in the second syllable, such as "heaven," "haven," "given," "never," and so forth. A well-known contraction is "flower"—with tacit acknowledgment of its French pedigree (*flor, flour, fleur*) and its prosodical relationship with such rhymes as hour–our (cf. higher–fire). Shakespeare contracted not only "flower" and "being" into one semeion each, but compressed into two semeia such words as "maidenhead" and "violet" ("maid'nhead," "vi'let"). In some cases, the strange evolution affecting *ve* has resulted in the formation of a new word, such as "o'er" instead of "over." Among time-honored slurrings is the curious case of "spiritual" contracted from four semeia (spir-it-u-al) to a disyllable sounding like something between "sprichal" and "spirchal," on the perfectly logical basis that if "spirit" is scanned, as it often is, monosyllabically (as happens with "merit" and "buried") and if, say, "actual" is scanned "actu'l," why not contract to one semeion each part of "spiritual" ("spir'tu'l")?

The vowels *u* and *e* in the unaccented second syllable of trochaic verbs are prone to be elided in participle forms ("murm'ring," "gath'ring," "gard'ning," etc.). Numerous other cases of elision, such as the loss of the *i* value in "-tion" (another obvious analogy with French), come readily to mind and need not be discussed here. In result, the employment of tilt and elision can make a perfect iambic tetrameter out of a sentence that as spoken fits no meter:

> watching the approaching flickering storm
> watching th'approaching flick'ring storm.

The beauty of the English elision lies neither in the brutal elimination of a syllable by an apostrophe nor in the recognition of an added semeion by leaving the word typographically intact, but in the delicate sensation of something being physically preserved by the voice at the very instant that it is metaphysically denied by the meter. Thus, the pleasure produced by a contraction or a liaison is the simultaneous awareness of the loss of a syllable on one level and its retention on another and the state of balance achieved between meter and rhythm. It is the perfect example of the possibility of eating one's cake and having it.

Indiscriminate apostrophization disfigures elision by trying to reconcile eye and ear and satisfying neither. Judging by a certain pentametric line in *The Canterbury Tales* ("Twenty bokes, clad in blak and reed"—"Prologue," l. 294), I suppose Chaucer pronounced "twenty" as "two-enty," as children still do today, but must a printer try to reproduce chance mannerisms or iron out blatant errors? Inexperienced Russian versifiers have been known to expand *oktyábr'* ("October") and *skiptr* ("scepter") to *ok-tyá-ber'* and *ski-pe-ter*—mere prosodic mistakes of no interest.

Elision, properly speaking, does not occur in Russian.

Faintly approaching it is the substitution in verse of a
"soft sign" (transliterated coincidentally by an apostrophe) for the valued *i* before a final vowel in such
endings as *-anie* and *-enie* (analogical to "-ion" endings
in English). Thus, the contraction of the three-syllabic
*tlénie* ("decomposition") to the disyllabic *tlén'e* (I repeat,
to avoid confusion, that the apostrophe here merely tran-
scribes the soft sign—a letter that looks somewhat like
a 6 in print or script) may be compared to the slurring of
the *i* in "lenient" or "onion." Pushkin and other poets of
his time wrote and pronounced *koy-kák* ("haphazardly")
for *kóe-kák*; and the archaic omission of the final vowel
in adjectives, which Pushkin permitted himself now and
then (*stárï gódï*, "olden times," and *táyna prélest'*,
"secret enchantment," for *stárïe gódï* and *táynaya
prélest'*), may be regarded as a crude form of elision.
Otherwise, such metrical pronunciations as *zháv'ronok*
for *zhávoronok* ("lark") and *dvoyúr'dnïy brat* for
*dvoyúrodnïy brat* ("first cousin") are but the blunders
of poetasters.

## 7. THE ORIGINATION OF METRICAL VERSE IN RUSSIA

*Iz pámyati izgrízli gódï,*
*Kto i za chtó v Hotíne pál;*
*No pérvïy zvúk Hotínskoy ódï*
*Nam pérvïm kríkom zhízni stál.*
— HODASEVICH (1938)*

Years have from memory eroded
Who perished at Hotin, and why;
But the Hotinian ode's first sound
For us became our life's first cry.

---

*This century has not yet produced any Russian poet surpassing
Vladislav Hodasevich (1886–1939). The best edition of his
poems is *Sobranie stihov*, ed. Nina Berberov (Munich, 1961).

In this section I am not concerned with the anonymous
remnants of medieval narrative poetry in Russia, the
unrhymed and nonmetrical recitatives, whose form,
botched by centuries of oral transmission, was, by the
eighteenth century, when the metrical system was first
borrowed from the West, incapable of providing individual talent with a diction and a technique:

> *Chelovécheskoe sérdtse nesmýslenno i neuímchivo:*
> *Prel'stílsya Adám so Évvoyu,*
> *Pozabíli zápoved' Bózhiyu,*
> *Vkusíli plóda vinográdnogo*
> *Ot dívnogo dréva velíkogo . . .*

Literal English translation:

> The human heart is unreasonable and uncontrollable:
> Adam was tempted, with Eve;
> They forgot God's commandment,
> They tasted the fruit of the grape
> From the wondrous great tree . . .

These lines (11–15) from a famous recitative piece entitled *The Tale of Grief and Ill-Fortune* (*Povest' o gore i
zloschastii*), written probably about 1625 and preserved
in a single eighteenth-century MS copy, afford a good example of a loose folk rhythm or ritual rhythm that had
flowed on for anything up to half a millennium, but that
in the age of Lomonosov had practically no effect at all on
the evolution of verse form in Russia. Patriotic scholars
have attempted to find a trochaic rhythm in short-line
Russian folk songs, but I cannot think of any such piece
following a regular tonic scheme before the eighteenth
century had set the metrical tune; the latter happened
to be congenial to national speech accentuation but was,
as most of modern Russian culture, a western European
grafting upon an organism that, in intrinsic poetical
power, surpassed the models stemming from eighteenth-
century Germany and France.

The origins of a national versification are seldom interesting. Prosody begins to matter only after poets have started to use it, and no poets were the makers of ponderous didactic doggerels who in the seventeenth century and on the threshold of the eighteenth century rhymed unscannable lines of random length, in an abruptly Westernized Russia, in an attempt to introduce a Polish system of syllabic verse, with strictly feminine rhyme, stumbling on in cacophonic couplets. Unendurable dullness settles upon him who peruses these imitations of structures, mediocre in themselves and completely alien to the rhythm of live Russian. His poor rewards are a few chance strains of trochaic lilt audible here and there in the otherwise amorphous heptasyllables (not counting the feminine terminals) of the learned monk, Feofán Prokopóvich (1681–1736), and a few curious samples of moralistic pieces, in ludicrously incorrect Russian, put together by German pedagogues peddling various metrical imitations at the Russian court.

By the third decade of the eighteenth century, the syllabic line that really threatened to stay was an uncouth thing of thirteen syllables (counting the obligative feminine terminal), with a caesura after the seventh syllable:

*Bezúmnïy prósit viná; zri! múdrost' p'yot vódu.*
The madman clamors for wine; see! wisdom drinks water.

The marks are there merely to show the accentuation of the Russian words; the English counterpart conforms exactly to the original. The order of stresses in the thirteener went in jumps and jolts and varied from line to line. The only rule (followed only by purists) was that the seventh, caesural, syllable must bear a beat. Another beat, the rhyme stress, fell on the twelfth syllable. It was on these two crutches that, as we shall presently see, a metrical form hobbled out of its syllabic prison and, casting away its props, suddenly began to dance.

In 1735, Vasiliy Trediakovski (1703–69), a wretched rhymester but a man of intuition and culture, published a muddled and yet rather remarkable *New and Brief Method of Russian Versemaking*, in which he proposed a theory of metrical versification applicable to Russian thirteeners and offered examples composed in accordance with this theory. His "Rule First" reads: "The Russian heroic line [or "Russian hexameter"] consists of thirteen syllables, or six feet." All these feet were, according to him, binaries,* of four species, iamb, trochee, "pyrrhic," and "spondee," placed in any order within the line, except that the last foot (forming the feminine rhyme) was always a trochee, and the third foot was never a trochee or a "pyrrhic."

Now—granted that other misguided metrists had also considered the "pyrrhic" and the "spondee" as "feet"—Trediakovski's system of dividing a thirteener into six feet might have been all right if he:

(1) Had postulated that one of the six feet—namely, one in the first section (of seven syllables)—should be a ternary foot (anapaest, amphibrach, dactyl, or any of the fancy varieties of the old pedants), or

(2) Had transformed his "heroic line" into a feminine-ending Alexandrine by moving the caesura one syllable proximad, thus cutting the line into 3+3 feet, with a stress on the sixth syllable, and discounting the unstressed last syllable of the second section, as being part of the (feminine) rhyme.

Instead, Trediakovski, in order to divide thirteen by six without remainder, followed what seemed to him a more scholarly course: he disregarded the seventh (stressed) syllable of the first (seven-syllable) section, calling it a hypercalectic syllable; i.e., a stressed stop (by analogy with the time-honored error of counting as a

---

*He denounced ternary feet because their use made an "unseemly scamper" of Russian verse!

caesural stop, and not as the normal ictus of a truncated dactylic foot, the third stress in the so-called elegiac pentameter (see p. 28).

According to his system, the following typically syllabic couplet would have to be scanned as a first line consisting of a medley of myths: two iambs, a pyrrhic, the caesural stop syllable, a spondee, an iamb, and a trochee; and a second line consisting of another assemblage: three iambs, the caesural stop syllable, two iambs, and a trochee:

$$
\begin{array}{c|c|c|c|c}
\cup \; \acute{} & \cup \; \acute{} & \cup \; \cup & \text{STOP} & \acute{} \; \acute{} \\
\text{The mad-} & \text{man cla-} & \text{mors for} & \text{wine;} & \text{see! wis-}
\end{array}
$$

$$
\begin{array}{c|c}
\cup \; \acute{} & \acute{} \; \cup \\
\text{dom drinks} & \text{water;}
\end{array}
$$

$$
\begin{array}{c|c|c|c|c}
\cup \; \acute{} & \cup \; \acute{} & \cup \; \acute{} & \text{STOP} & \cup \; \acute{} \\
\text{The pant-} & \text{ing rake} & \text{arrives} & \text{late;} & \text{success}
\end{array}
$$

$$
\begin{array}{c|c}
\cup \; \acute{} & \acute{} \; \cup \\
\text{is thrift's} & \text{daughter.}
\end{array}
$$

Trediakovski continues thus: "However, the most perfect and best verse is a line that consists solely or mainly of trochees, whereas a line consisting solely or mainly of iambs is a very bad one."

The first part of this passage was an epoch-making statement. Trediakovski's attack on the iamb is readily explained by the fact that he so labeled an arbitrarily chosen component of a heterogeneous line broken by a gap no iamb could bridge. Well might he find fault with such doggerel rhythms as I have mimicked above.

It is also of no consequence that he saw his trochaic line as a combination of trochees and "pyrrhics," with the beat of the seventh syllable not counted as part of a foot. This omission did not distort the trochaic meter, for the simple reason that what he omitted was really a trochee truncated by a masculine termination. His faulty theories were redeemed by the "elegies" he submitted as examples; they possess no literary merit but contain the first trochees deliberately composed in Russian, and prefigure, if not inaugurate, the metrical system.

His *Elegy* II (1735), ll. 79–82, reads:

> *Dolgovátoe litsó i rumyáno bílo,*
> *Beliznóyu zhe svoéy vsyó prevoskhodílo;*
> *Búd' na bélost' zrísh' litsá, to liléi zryátsya,*
> *Na rumyánost' búde zrísh', rózï to krasyátsya.*

> Elongated was her face and of rosy brightness,
> While surpassing everything by its lily whiteness;
> When its whiteness you regard, lilies it discloses,
> When its color you regard, lovely are its roses.

In each of these lines the thirteen-syllable abomination of the schoolman was metamorphosed, and what emerged was not one metrical line, as Trediakovski thought, but two trippingly scudded verses—a trochaic tetrameter (with a masculine termination) and a trochaic trimeter (including a feminine rhyme at the end):

> When its whiteness you regard,
> Lilies it discloses;
> When its color you regard,
> Lovely are its roses.

The birth of the iambic tetrameter, to which we now must turn, was not a consequence of the breaking up of the Russian heroic line—a trochaic potentiality to begin with. The favorite meter of later poets is heard raising its melodious voice now and then in syllabic verse as an undifferentiated variation of the nonasyllable. Thus, in a "cantata" consisting of syllabic lines of varying length, mostly unscannable, that Trediakovski, in his premetrical period, knocked together on the occasion of Empress Anna's coronation (July 30, 1730), there is an accidental modicum of adjacent metrical verses such as:

> *Vospléshchem grómko i rukámi,*
> *Zaskáchem véselo nogámi . . .*

> With hands, too, loudly let's be clapping,
> With feet let's merrily be hopping . . .

which are ordinary iambic tetrameters scudded on the third foot.* But the introduction of the iambic tetrameter as an emphatic and conscious act, and the establishment of a clearly and correctly expressed metrical system of Russian prosody, were not owing to Trediakovski. He may be deemed the sponsor of the trochee. The godfather of the iambic tetrameter is the famous reformer Lomonosov.

In September, 1739, in a "Letter about the Rules of Russian Versification" (first published in 1778), which Mihail Lomonosov (1711–65) sent (from the German university town of Freiburg, where he was studying metallurgy) to the members of a philologic committee attached to the Academy of Sciences in St. Petersburg, he advocated the total adoption of the metrical system and added as a separate illustrative item the first Russian poem, an ode, entirely and deliberately composed in iambic tetrameters. This is the *Ode to the Sovereign of Blessed Memory Anna Ioannovna on the Victory over the Turks and Tatars and on the Taking of Hotin* (or Khotin, a fortress in Bessarabia, SW Russia, formerly an old Genoese citadel, restored by the Turks with the assistance of French engineers, and stormed by Russian troops on Aug. 19, 1739). The MS of this piece, now known as *The Hotinian Ode*, is lost. Scattered fragments of its initial text are quoted by Lomonosov in his manual,

---

*Just as in the Northumbrian Psalter, of four and a half centuries ago, we find, here and there, iambic tetrameters, some of which are scudded on the third foot, such as "Of moúth of chílder and soukánd [sucklings]"—Psalm 8, l. 5. See also the beginning of the so-called "Tale of a Usurer" in the *Sunday Homilies* of c. 1330, in which a Scud II occurs:

> "An hóli mán biyónd the sé
> Was bíschop of a grét cité."

*A Brief Guide to Rhetoric*, 1744 (pars. 53, 54, 79, 100, 105, 112) and 1748 (pars. 68, 163, 203). The *Ode* was published by Lomonosov, in a revised edition (revised both in matter and manner, to judge by the fragments in his *Guide to Rhetoric*), only in 1751 (*Collection of Various Works by Lomonosov*), though it seems to have been known to the curious long before that. It is in stanzas of ten iambic tetrameters rhymed babaccedde (as usual in my notation, the vowels represent feminine rhymes). In this particular ode the rhyme scheme reverses the feminine-masculine sequence (ababeeciic) of the usual French ode of ten-verse stanzas (inaugurated by Ronsard, popularized by Malherbe), which Lomonosov used as a stanza model, and of the later odes by Lomonosov himself and by Derzhavin, his great successor.

In its preserved form of 1751 *The Hotinian Ode* begins:

> *Vostórg vnezápnïy úm pleníl,*
> *Vedyót na vérh gorí vïsókoy*
> *Gde vétr v lesáh shumét' zabíl;*
> 4 *V dolíne tishiná glubókoy;*
> *Vnimáya néchto, klyúch molchít,*
> *Kotórïy zavsegdá zhurchít*
> *I s shúmom vníz s holmóv stremítsya.*
> 8 *Lavróvï v'yútsya tám ventsí,*
> *Tam slúh speshít vo vsé kontsí;*
> *Daléche dím v polyáh kurítsya.*

> A sudden rapture thralls the mind,
> leads to the top of a high mountain
> where wind in woods forgets to sound;
> 4 there is a hush in the deep valley;
> to something listing silent is
> the spring that murmured all the time
> and down the hills with noise went surging;
> 8 there, laurel crowns are being wound;
> there, hastes a rumor to all points;
> smoke in the fields afar is rising.

The fountain is Castalia, on Mt. Parnassus.

This 1751 version of *The Hotinian Ode* has rather frequent scuds—for example, in II (a modulation that Lomonosov held in better favor than did Pushkin):

> 41 *Ne méd' li v chréve Étnï rzhyót*
> *I, s séroyu kipyá, klokóchet?*
> *Ne ád li tyázhki úzï rvyót*
> *I chélyusti razínut' hóchet?*

> Does brass in Etna's belly neigh
> And bubble, with the sulphur boiling?
> Is Hades tearing heavy chains,
> Endeavoring his jaws to open?

I have kept the literal sense and the rhythm but have sacrificed to their retention the alternate, masculine and feminine, rhymes. The word "neigh" is taken in the old sense, both English and Russian, meaning "to make a loud, harsh, jarring, and jeering sound." (In modern Russian *rzhanie*, "neighing," would apply only to the voice of a horse, or, vulgarly, to a succession of human guffaws.)

The rhyme sequence babaccedde in the odic stanza of ten lines (as used in *The Hotinian Ode*, ll. 41–50, in which the terminals are *rzhyót, klokóchet, rvyót, hóchet, rabí, rví, brosáet, naród, bolót, derzáet*;* the cc rhyme here is a poor one, as will be explained further) follows not the musical French alternation that begins on a feminine rhyme and ends in a masculine one (ababeeciic, as used, for instance, by Malherbe and Boileau), but German models in the odic department (in other respects, imitations of French, of course), which also provided Lomonosov with the predominance of scudless lines that he advocated in his early metrical theories. The babaccedde alternations are found, for example, in an ode by Johann Christian Günther (1695–1723), *Auf*

---

*In English: neighs, bubbles, tears, wishes (all verbs), slave (fem. gen.), fosses, throws, people, marshes (gen.), dares.

*den zwischen Ihre Röm. Kaiserl. Majestät und der
Pforte An. 1718 geschlossenen Frieden*, a formidable en-
gine of five hundred verses dedicated to the peace concluded between Austria and Turkey (July 21, 1718). It
has less than twenty per cent of scudded lines (not
counting a few semiscuds). For example, ll. 11–20:

> Die Walstatt ist noch nass und lau
> Und stinkt nach Türken, Schand und Leichen.
> Wer sieht nicht die verstopfte Sau
> Von Äsern faul und mühsam schleichen?
> Und dennoch will das deutsche Blut
> Den alten Kirchhof feiger Wut
> An jungen Lorbeern fruchtbar machen,
> Und gleichwohl hört der dicke Fluss
> Des Sieges feurigen Entschluss
> Aus Mörsern und Kartaunen krachen.

Using my modification of the Belian system of notation
(see p. 15), we have:

| I | II | III | IV |
|---|----|-----|----|
| o | o | o | o |
| o | o | o | o |
| o | x | o | o |
| o | o | o | o |
| o | o | o | o |
| o | o | o | o |
| o | o | o | o |
| o | o | o | o |
| o | o | x | o |
| o | x | o | o |

There are a Scud II in ll. 13 and 20 and a III in l. 19.

*The Hotinian Ode*, although reversing the French
order of rhymes (followed by Lomonosov in his later
odes and in an earlier effort of his, in trochaic tetrameter,
October, 1738, an imitation of an ode by Fénélon), contains in the quoted lines clumsy echoes of the imagery in
the third stanza of Boileau's *Ode sur la prise de Namur*
(1693; an imitation in style of Malherbe's ode *Au Roy*

*Henry le Grand, sur la prise de Marseille,*\* composed
1596, pub. 1630), ll. 21–30:

> Est-ce Apollon, et Neptune
> Qui sur ces Rocs sourcilleux
> Ont, compagnons de fortune,
> Basti ces murs orgueilleux?
> De leur enceinte fameuse
> La Sambre unie à la Meuse
> Deffend le fatal abord,
> Et par cent bouches horribles
> L'airain sur ces monts terribles
> Vômit le fer, et la mort.†

Among the fragments (1744–48) of *The Hotinian Ode*
we find such archaic lines as:

> *Pretít' ne mógut ógn', vodá,*
> *Orlítsa kak parít tudá*

which can be rendered in sixteenth-century English:

> Her can ne flame, ne flood retard
> When soars the eagless thitherward.

Like all Lomonosov's verses, *The Hotinian Ode* has
little poetic merit, but prepares the advent of Derzhavin,
who was the first real poet in Russia. It should be noted
that despite the clumsiness of Lomonosov's idiom, with
its obscure banalities and perilous inversions of speech,

---

\*That particular ode by Malherbe, and Boileau's poem, happen
to be not in octosyllabics (as French odes generally are) but
heptasyllabics, thus corresponding, in Russian or English, not
to iambic but to trochaic tetrameters. The first Russian ode
(1734), Trediakovski's *Ode on the Surrender of the Town of
Gdansk* (*Oda o sdache goroda Gdanska*, referring to Danzig
taken by the Russians in a war with Poland, 1734), in syllabic
verse, is also an imitation of Boileau's piece, and was present
at the back of Lomonosov's mind in the course of composition.
†The insipid rhymes *sourcilleux–orgueilleux* and *horribles–
terribles* contrast oddly with the rich rhymes *Neptune–
fortune* and *fameuse–Meuse*, both of which, however, were at
least a century old in 1693. The two gods mentioned helped to
rebuild the walls of Troy.

*43*

his iambic tetrameter already includes all the modulations that Derzhavin, Batyushkov, Zhukovski, and Pushkin brought to such perfection. At first Lomonosov deemed scuds good only for light verses, but in the mid-1740's gave in and sparingly used all the types of scuds we know. He was the first Russian to allow cross rhyme.

To be quite exact, actual priority in the inauguration of the Russian iambic tetrameter should be given not to the fragments of *The Hotinian Ode* found scattered through the *Rhetoric*, but to a sample of this meter supplied by Lomonosov in his letter of 1739 (and marked by a subtle, perhaps unconscious, use of the same "fairface" imagery as that in Trediakovski's sample trochaic lines of 1735). This very first Russian iambic tetrameter goes:

*Beléet búdto snég litsóm . . .*

in which *Beleet*=he, she, or it "looks white," or "is fairskinned," or "whitens" (intr.); *budto*="as if," "similar to"; *sneg*="snow"; *litsom*=instr. of *litso*, "face"; corresponding to "in face" or "of face." The closest translation allowed by the meter would be:

Appeárs as whíte of fáce as snów . . .

A little further, in the same letter, Lomonosov devises an example of a scud in the regular iambic tetrameter (at the time he approved of these "pyrrhic" liberties only in "songs"):

*Tsvetí, rumyánets umnozháyte!*

The first word means "flowers," the second, "rosy complexion" (cf. Trediakovski's less colloquial *rumyánost'*), and the third is "augment" (pl. imp.).

Ye bloóms, augmént your colorátion.

The samples of other meters that Lomonosov gives in his letter look similar, as if stills were taken of them while they hovered above an unknown context; but one

of his illustrations—namely, that of a dactylic hexameter
—makes at least pleasing sense:

> *V'yótsya krugámi zmiyá po travé, obnovívshis' v*
> *rasséline . . .*

> Windeth in circles a snake through the grass, in
> a crack having molted . . .

I have not managed to keep the dactylic ending, but the
feminine one is the one used by Zhukovski and Pushkin
in this measure.

Of tremendous interest to the student of Russian
prosody is a forty-four-line song (beginning *Gde ni
gulyáyu, ni hozhú,* "Wherever ramble I or go," *Grust'
prevelíkuyu terplyú,* "I bear immeasurable woe"),
which one of Boileau's Russian followers, Aleksandr
Sumarokov (1718–77), produced in 1759, when, with
Trediakovski's trochees and Lomonosov's iambs, the
metrical system had triumphed over the syllabic one.
This lyrical poem, a stylized peasant girl's love chant, is
of little artistic worth but reveals a singular purity of
phrasing, superior to the more imaginative but also
more awkward idiom of Lomonosov. In it Sumarokov
attempts to blend the liberties of stress, characteristic of
the syllabic octosyllable, with a scansion that is practically an iambic one. To an iambically trained ear catch-
ing the rhythm of the first two verses, the entire piece
sounds exactly like the Russian counterpart of an English
poem in which the first foot, and the first foot only, is being boldly tilted in every line. There are as many as
twenty duplex tilts, and even one long tilt, in it, while
all the rest of the lines are split-tilted with various de-
grees of sharpness. Of the duplex tilts only one belongs
to the small group of "neutral" words (l. 32, *Ili on
póverhu plïvyót,* "Whether upon the surface floats").
The others are such disyllables as *vésel* (l. 23) and *túzhit*
(l. 29):

> *Vesel li tî, kogdá so mnóy?*
> Merry are you when you're with me?

> *Tuzhit li v tóy on storoné?*
> Grieving is he in yonder land?

The long tilt is in l. 18, *Sdelalsya míl mne kak dushá*, "Lovable grew he as my soul." Unfortunately, Sumarokov's tilts proved stillborn. This and other poems of his were rejected as syllabic fossils by the next generation, and not a single Russian poet, except one or two innovators of today, ever dared use the free duplex tilt that had been accidentally introduced by the rhythm of Sumarokov's curious experiment in meter.

### 8. DIFFERENCE IN MODULATION

The first thing that strikes the student visually when he compares Russian verse structures to English ones is the lesser number of words that go to form a Russian line metrically identical to an English one. This feature is owing both to an actual preponderance of polysyllables in the Russian language and to the inflective lengthening of its monosyllables such as nouns and verbs. Certain disyllabic forms, such as most nonmasculine nouns of two syllables, remain of that length despite inflective alterations (except in the instrumental plural, when a syllable is added); and, on the other hand, certain participial adjectives are capable of such a hypertrophy of caudal segments as to make them uncontainable within a tetrametrical line.

Generally speaking, it is only the lower words, such as prepositions and conjunctions, not affected by inflection, that can be readily compared to their English counterparts as represented in verse. But even this is sometimes not possible, since another extreme is obtained in Russian through the scriptorial dwindling of three common Russian words to metrical nothings in the case of the prepositions *k* ("to"), *s* ("with"), and *v* ("in"), which as such (i.e., not lengthened to *ko*, *so*, *vo*, as they are for euphonic reasons before certain words) are not monosyllables at all, but ethereal consonants that are allowed a discrete existence only by grammatical courtesy. I hope that in the revised, and romanized, Russian script of the future these consonantal prepositions will be connected with the mother word by means of a hyphen (*v-dushe*, "in the soul").

The predominance of polysyllables in Russian verse (as compared to the prodigious quantity of monosyllabic adjectives and verbs in English) is basically owing to the absence of monosyllabic adjectives* in Russian (there is only one: *zloy*, "wicked") and a comparative paucity of monosyllabic past tenses among the verbs (e.g., *pel*, "sang"), all of which, adjectives and verbs alike, are lengthened by number, declension, conjugation, and nonmasculine gender. Inflection also results in the comparatively rare occurrence of lower words corresponding to those that speckle English verse and pullulate in English speech, although of course, in a stanza or short poem in which the notions of altitude, confrontation, or distance happen to predominate, the occurrence of *na* ("on"), *nad* ("above"), *pod* ("under"), *pred* or *pered* ("before"), *ot* ("from"), *do* ("to"), and so forth would be as frequent as in English. And last but not least, the quantity of words in the line is affected by the nonexistence of Russian words exactly corresponding to the English definite and indefinite articles.

In result of all these facts, a Russian who wants to say "the man" uses only one word, but this word is a trisyllable: *chelovék*. Its dative, "to a man" or "to the man" or "to man," is *chelovéku* or *k cheloveku*—four syllables. *Dushá* is "soul"; and "in the soul" is *v dushé*—two sylla-

*See Author's Note, p. vii.

bles. Very seldom, in translations from Russian into English and vice versa, can one monosyllabic noun be rendered by another. Some comfort is afforded in this respect by the coincidences *dni* and "days," *sni* and "dreams," *mir* and "peace," and a few others, but the singular *son* is "a dream" or "the dream"—two syllables —and *sna* is "of the dream"—three syllables. And although we can find quite a few long adjectives in English to match those of five, six, and seven syllables that are so abundant in Russian, it will be immediately clear from a comparative study of serious English and Russian poets, especially those of the nineteenth century, that because of associations with the burlesque genre the lyrical English poet will use conspicuous polysyllables warily, sparingly, or not at all, whereas the Russian lyricist, especially one of Pushkin's time, who has no such worries, will feel a natural melodic association between, say, the melancholy of love and polysyllabic epithets. In consequence, the mark of a first-rate performer of the time—the 1820's, when the Russian iambic tetrameter was at its highest level of popularity with minor and major poets*—was the two-word or three-word technique; i.e., the art of making a minimum of words shape the line. This I term the "full line." The natural colloquial falling into place of large words coin-

---

*A decline of poetry set in after the time of Tyutchev (1803–73), despite the continued existence of two other major poets, Nekrasov (1821–77) and Fet (1820–92), neither of them a master of iambic tetrameter. The revival of poetry in the first two decades of this century was also marked by a revival of the meter in question; but a tendency has arisen among serious poets in recent years to give the form a greater concentration of meaning, sometimes at the expense of melody, owing perhaps to one's irritation by the upstart modulations used by a generation of rhymesters who easily caught the scudding knack after Belïy's work (1910), which found in scudding a separative agent to distinguish genius from mediocrity in the untheorizing past.

cides with an absence of gap fillers and lame monosyllables and results in a surge of scuds, so that, in the nineteenth century, a high rate of scuds became a sign of expert handling in matters of poetical idiom.

Masculine full lines in *EO* are limited to twenty-one combinations of three words and to six of two words (the additional possibility 1 + 7, involving the unpleasant I–II scud, was not used in Pushkin's day). The following are random samples typical of Pushkinian intonations in *EO*:

2+5+1: *Egó toskúyushchuyu lén'* [One : VIII : 8; which means "his fretting indolence" (acc.)]

2+4+2: *Vdalí Itálii svoéy* [One : VIII : 14; which means "far from his Italy"]

3+4+1: *Zhelániy svoevól'niy róy* [One : XXXII : 8; which is best rendered by the eighteenth-century French "Des désirs le volage essaim"]

1+4+3: *Chtob epigráfï razbirát'* [One : VI : 4; which means "in order to make out epigraphs"]

7+1: *Zakonodátel'nitse zál* [Eight : XXVIII : 7; which means "in the legislatrix of salons"]

6+2: *Ostanovílasya oná* [Five : XI : 14; the first word means "stopped," and the second "she" (one wonders by means of what miraculous circumlocution an English versifier might manage to compose a double-scud iambic tetrameter merely meaning "she stopped")]

The number of two-word or three-word lines is about thirty per cent in *EO*, to judge by a number of random samplings. In samplings from English poets, it rises from zero to barely five per cent. Among poets who use full lines more often than most English poets do, we find:

2+3+3: Suspends uncertaine victorie [Donne, *The Extasie*, l. 14]

2+6: Upon Impossibility [Marvell, *The Definition of Love*, l. 4]

4+2+2: Magnanimous Despair alone [ibid., l. 5]

and so forth; but in romantic poets, a natural contempt for Hudibrastics restrains somewhat the urge toward the formation of full lines. *

We can now sum up the main differences in modulation between English and Russian iambic tetrameters as used by major poets. †

### English

(1) Scudless lines predominate over scudded ones in any given poem. In exceptional cases, at the maximal frequency of scudded lines, their number is about equal to that of scudless lines.

(2) Sequences of scudded lines are never very long. Five or six in a row occur very seldom. As a rule, they merely dot the background of scudless series instead of forming sustained patterns from line to line.

(3) Scuds are frequently associated with weak monosyllables, duplex tilts, and scudded rhymes (Scud IV).

(4) Scud I and Scud II occur about as frequently as Scud III but often tend to predominate, with Scud IV comparatively a rarity. The line is weighted accentually toward its end.

---

*Paradoxically enough, it is to English that we must go to find instances, in minor poetry, of a tetrameter made up entirely of one word. I am thinking of T. S. Eliot's *Mr. Eliot's Sunday Morning Service*, which begins with the (apparently, jocular) line: "Polyphiloprogenitive." This, of course, can be (but never has been) duplicated in Russian; e.g., *polupereimenovát'* (which means "to rename incompletely" and illustrates the additional metrical feat, impossible in English, of obtaining three scuds in a row instead of the scud, semiscud, accented stress-scudded terminal of the English example).

†Among major Russian poets, the greatest masters in the form were, in the nineteenth century, Pushkin and Tyutchev and, in the twentieth, Blok and Hodasevich. Lermontov's iambic tetrameters do not reflect his genius at its best, even in his celebrated *Demon*. Baratïnski and Yazïkov are often mentioned with the major poets as tetrametric performers, but the first was definitely a minor poet and the second a mediocre one.

(5) Feminine rhymes are scarce, insipid, or burlesque.

(6) Elisions are more or less frequent.

### Russian

(1) Scudded lines greatly predominate over scudless ones.

(2) Scuds often form linked patterns from line to line, for half a dozen lines in a row and up to twenty or more. Scudless lines rarely occur in sequences above two or three lines in a row.

(3) Scuds are frequently associated with the unaccented syllables of long words. Apart from the few exceptions noted, there are no duplex tilts. Rhymes are not scudded (absence of Scud IV).

(4) Scud III greatly predominates over other scuds. The line is weighted accentually toward its beginning.

(5) Feminine rhymes are as frequent as masculine ones and add extrametrical music to the verse.

(6) There are, strictly speaking, no elisions of any kind.

#### 9. EXAMPLES OF MODULATIONS

English meter came into being almost four centuries before Russian meter did. In both cases, modulation was born with the measure. Among the tetrameters of Chaucer's *The Hous of Fame* (1383–84), there are trochaic and iambic lines that contain all the scuds of later poets, although as usual with English poets the basic pattern is the scudless line and not, as in Russian, the third-foot scud. In *The Hous of Fame* we find a few third-foot scuds (l. 352, "Though hit be kevered with the mist," or l. 1095, "Here art poetical be shewed"), a few second-foot scuds (l. 70, "That dwelleth in a cave of stoon"), a few combinations of second-foot and third-foot scuds (l. 223, "And prevely took arrivage"). It displays such rhythmic formulas as, for example, the famous one based on two sonorous names (l. 589, "Ne Romulus, ne Ganymede"), which probably every English poet who favored the tetrameter has used once or twice, down to our own times. Even tilts are present (l. 605, " 'Gladly,' quod I. 'Now wel,' quod he"), but they are still rare, for when faced with the necessity of using an initial strong monosyllable or a strongheaded disyllable, old poets often preferred to switch for a verse or two from the dominant iambic meter to a trochaic one (i.e., to a line shorter by one, initial, syllable) rather than to tilt the iambic foot.

It is not my intention here to outline, even cursorily, the history of the English iamb. But a few disjointed observations may be of some use.

I think that on the whole the iambic tetrameter has fared better in Russia than in England. The Russian iambic tetrameter is a solid, polished, disciplined thing, with rich concentrated meaning and lofty melody fused in an organic entity: it has said in Russian what the pentameter has said in English, and the hexameter in French. Now, on the other hand, the English iambic tetrameter is a hesitating, loose, capricious form, always in danger of having its opening semeion chopped off, or of being diluted by a recurrent trimeter, or of developing a cadential lilt. The English form has been instrumental in producing a quantity of admirable short poems but has never achieved anything approaching, either in sheer length or artistic importance, a stanzaic romance comparable to *Eugene Onegin*. The trouble is that with the English iambic tetrameter the pendulum of its purpose swings between two extremes—stylized primitivity and ornate burlesque. The scudless or nearly scudless iambic tetrameter has been consistently looked upon by English poets and critics as something characteristic of the "folk ditty" and conducive to an effect of "simplicity" and "sincerity." Now, this kind of thing is a serious obstacle to the evolution of an art form. I am aware that the specious terms "simplicity" and "sincerity" are constantly employed in a commendatory sense by well-meaning teachers of literature. Actually, of course, no matter how "simple" the result looks, true art is never simple, being always an elaborate, magical deception, even if it seems to fit in well with an author's temperament, ideas, biography, and so forth. Art is a magical deception, as all nature is magic and deception. To speak of a "sincere" poem or picture is about the same thing as to call "sincere" a bird's mating dance or a caterpillar's mimetic behavior.

By the seventeenth century, the English iambic tetrameter, in the hands of some performers of genius, becomes capable of elaborate music while treating frivolous as well as metaphysical themes. But at this historical point a disaster takes place. The emancipation of the iambic tetrameter in England becomes associated with the tendency toward Hudibrastics. Even the exceptionally artistic poetry of Marvell tends fatally to lapse into the atrocious genre associated with Samuel Butler's burlesque. This kind of stuff—the boisterous and obscure topical satire, the dismally comic, mock-heroic poem, the social allusion sustained through hundreds of rhymed couplets, the academic tour de force, and the coy fugitive verses—is something intrinsically inartistic and antipoetical since its enjoyment presupposes that Reason is somehow, in the long run, superior to Imagination, and that both are less important than a man's religious or political beliefs. It has nothing to do with wit, but has a great deal to do with a certain persistent strain of mental archness that in modern times is so painfully audible in much of Mr. T. S. Eliot's work.

The sad fact is thus that the English iambic tetrameter, despite the genius of some great poets who made it sing and shimmer, has been maimed for life by certain, still thriving, trends and forms such as light verse (e.g., more or less elegant rearrangements of conventional images and ideas), the burlesque or mock-heroic genre (a dreadful category that includes political and scholarly romps), didactic verse (comprising not only catalogues of natural phenomena but also various "meditations" and "hymns" reflecting the standard ideas and traditions of organized religious groups), and various junctions and overlappings of these three main varieties.

This is not to say that there are not many tetrametric masterpieces in English. Some of the following samples, to which diagrams of modulations are appended, come from immortal productions unsurpassed in any language by poems belonging to the same category. These samples are followed by diagrams of *EO* rhythms.

In all the diagrams, a scudless foot is designated by an o and a scudded one by an x. Semiscuds (such as the word "when") are treated as regular beats. Duplex tilts are italicized in the text (e.g., in the second sample, l. 6). Split tilts (e.g., in the same sample, l. 5) are not italicized. False spondees (ibid., l. 2) are not marked in the diagrams, even when so topheavy as to border on the split tilt (e.g., in the sixth sample, l. 8, or in the sixteenth, l. 1).

1. Henry Howard, Earl of Surrey (1517?–47), *The Lover Describeth His Restless State*:

| I | II | III | IV | | |
|---|----|-----|----|---|---|
| o | o | o | o | 1 | As oft as I behold, and see |
| o | o | x | o | | The sovereign beauty that me bound; |
| o | o | o | o | | The nigher my comfort is to me, |
| o | o | o | o | | Alas! the fresher is my wound. |
| o | o | o | o | | As flame doth quench by rage of fire, |
| o | o | o | o | | And running streams consume by rain; |
| o | o | o | o | | So doth the sight that I desire |
| o | o | o | o | | Appease my grief and deadly pain. |

| | I | II | III | IV |
|---|---|---|---|---|
| Like as the fly that see'th the flame, | x | o | o | o |
| And thinks to play her in the fire; | o | o | x | o |
| That found her woe, and sought her game | o | o | o | o |
| Where grief did grow by her desire. | o | o | o | o |
| First when I saw those crystal streams, | o | o | o | o |
| 14  Whose beauty made my mortal wound . . . | o | o | o | o |

In this poem of forty-five lines, with from twenty-six to thirty-one words in each of its nine quatrains, there is only one word that has more than two syllables. In the fourteen lines given above, there are ninety-seven words, a number that is interesting to compare with the eighty words in a reasonably well-scudded English sample or with the Russian average of about fifty in a fourteen-line stanza of *EO*.

II. William Shakespeare (1564–1616), Sonnet CXLV (1609):

| | I | II | III | IV |
|---|---|---|---|---|
| 1  Those lips that Love's own hand did make | o | o | o | o |
| Breathed forth the sound that said "I hate" | o | o | o | o |
| To me that languish'd for her sake; | o | o | x | o |
| But when she saw my woeful state, | o | o | o | o |
| Straight in her heart did mercy come, | x | o | o | o |
| *Chiding* that tongue that ever sweet | x | o | o | o |
| Was used in giving gentle doom, | o | o | o | o |
| And taught it thus anew to greet; | o | o | o | o |
| "I hate" she alter'd with an end | o | o | x | o |
| That follow'd it as gentle day | o | o | o | o |
| Doth follow night, who, like a fiend, | o | o | x | o |
| From heaven to hell is flown away; | o | o | o | o |
| "I hate" from hate away she threw, | o | o | o | o |
| 14     And saved my life, *saying* "not you." | o | o | x | o |

In this elegant little sonnet (Shakespeare's only tetrametric one) the reader should note the comparatively high rate of scudding and, in the last line, the comparatively rare third-foot duplex tilt, here eased in by means of a concettic alliteration.

55

| I | II | III | IV | |
|---|----|-----|----|---|
| | | | | III. John Donne (1572–1631), *The Extasie* (pub. 1633): |
| o | o | x | o | 37 A single violet transplant, |
| o | o | x | o | The strength, the colour, and the size, |
| o | o | o | o | (All which before was poore, and scant,) |
| o | o | x | o | Redoubles still, and multiplies. |
| o | o | o | o | When love, with one another so |
| x | x | o | o | Interinanimates two soules, |
| o | o | o | o | That abler soule, which thence doth flow, |
| o | o | x | o | Defects of lonelinesse controules. |
| o | o | o | o | Wee then, who are this new soule, know, |
| o | o | o | o | Of what we are compos'd, and made. |
| o | x | o | o | For, th'Atomies of which we grow, |
| o | o | o | o | Are soules, whom no change can invade. |
| o | o | o | o | But O alas, so long, so farre |
| o | o | o | o | 50 Our bodies why do wee forbeare? |

A certain interesting eccentricity marks the rhythm of Donne, who has been somewhat overrated in recent years by lovers of religious verse. I have been slightly influenced in the choice of this particular passage by the presence of the very rare variation I+II, which, however, is a little impaired by the possibility of substituting a secondary accent for the second scud. There are plums in the rest of the pie; e.g., l. 29, "This Extasie doth unperplex," = II+III, and l. 66, "T'affections, and to faculties," = II+IV. The apostrophization of the ugly and trite elision in the second example is a mannerism of the time.

| I | II | III | IV | |
|---|----|-----|----|---|
| | | | | IV. John Milton (1608–74), *L'Allegro* (c. 1640): |
| o | o | o | o | 103 She was pincht, and pull'd she sed, |
| o | o | o | o | And he by Friars Lanthorn led |
| o | o | o | o | Tells how the drudging Goblin swet, |
| o | o | o | o | To ern his Cream-bowle duly set, |
| x | o | o | o | When in one night, ere glimps of morn, |
| o | o | o | o | His shadowy Flale hath thresh'd the Corn |
| o | o | o | o | That ten day-labourers could not end, |
| o | o | o | o | Then lies him down the Lubbar fend. |

| | I | II | III | IV |
|---|---|---|---|---|
| And stretch'd out all the Chimney's length, | o | o | o | o |
| Basks at the fire his hairy strength; | x | o | o | o |
| And Crop-full out of dores he flings, | o | x | o | o |
| Ere the first Cock his Mattin rings. | x | o | o | o |
| Thus don the Tales, to bed they creep, | o | o | o | o |
| 116 By whispering Windes soon lull'd asleep. | o | o | o | o |

It is not easy to find a sustained sequence of iambic tetrameters in Milton, who deliberately interrupts their flow by beheading the iamb every time it begins to domineer. Cadential verse for him, as for Coleridge and Keats, was a great and fertile temptation. This extract from a resplendent masterpiece (l. 112 is one of the best in English poetry) is not very abundantly scudded, but extra modulation is achieved by means of the contractions so characteristic of Milton's style: l. 108, "His shadowy Flale . . ."; l. 109, "That ten day-labourers . . ."; and l. 116, "By whispering Windes . . ."

v. Samuel Butler (1612–80), *Hudibras*, pt. I (pub. 1662), can. I:

| | I | II | III | IV |
|---|---|---|---|---|
| 187 For his Religion it was fit | o | o | o | o |
| To match his Learning and his Wit: | o | o | x | o |
| 'Twas Presbyterian true blew, | x | o | x | o |
| For he was of that stubborn Crew | o | x | o | o |
| Of Errant Saints, whom all men grant | o | o | o | o |
| To be the true Church Militant: | o | o | o | x |
| Such as do build their Faith upon | x | o | o | o |
| The holy Text of Pike and Gun; | o | o | o | o |
| Decide all Controversies by | o | x | o | x |
| Infallible Artillery; | o | x | o | x |
| And prove their Doctrine Orthodox | o | o | o | x |
| By Apostolick Blows and Knocks; | x | o | o | o |
| Call Fire and Sword and Desolation, | o | o | x | o |
| 200 A godly-thorough-Reformation . . . | o | o | x | o |

*Hudibras* teeters, of course, on the verge of jingle; in fact, it is the very parade of this teetering that barely saves it from hopeless topicality; but I give a sample of the stuff because it displays one of the standard uses—the journalistic, mock-heroic genre—to which English and German satirists have put the most poetical of meters. The passage is scudded ostentatiously and vulgarly (a symptom of this is the frequency of IV). A rich scudding of iambic tetrameters is fatally associated in the English mind with jocose forms of minor poetry and with the same suggestion of verbal intemperance that makes the fancy rhyme odious in English.

VI. Andrew Marvell (1621–78), *To His Coy Mistress* (pub. 1681):

| I | II | III | IV | | |
|---|----|-----|----|--|--|
| o | o | o | o | 1 | Had we but World enough, and Time, |
| o | o | o | o | | This coyness Lady were no crime. |
| o | o | o | o | | We would sit down, and think which way |
| o | o | o | o | | To walk, and pass our long Loves Day. |
| x | o | o | o | | Thou by the Indian Ganges side |
| o | o | x | o | | Should'st Rubies find: I by the Tide |
| o | o | o | o | | Of Humber would complain. I would |
| o | o | o | o | | Love you ten years before the Flood: |
| o | x | o | o | | And you should if you please refuse |
| x | o | x | o | | Till the Conversion of the Jews. |
| o | x | o | o | | My vegetable Love should grow |
| x | o | o | o | | *Vaster* than Empires, and more slow. |
| o | o | o | o | | An hundred years should go to praise |
| o | x | o | o | 14 | Thine Eyes, and on thy Forehead Gaze. |

Note the modulations in the second part of this passage. It comes from one of the greatest English short poems. I think that the "you" after the tilted "Love" in l. 8 rates half a scud, while the next one does not. Of the hundreds of English tetrameters I have examined, this—and certain sequences in Cotton and, alas, Samuel Butler—are closest in melodic figures to those so typical of Pushkin and his contemporaries, though still falling short of the Russian predilection for the rapid ripple of Scud III.

vii. Charles Cotton (1630–87), *The New Year* (pub. 1689):

| | | I | II | III | IV |
|---|---|---|---|---|---|
| 25 | And all the moments open are | o | o | o | o |
| | To the exact discoverer; | x | o | o | x |
| | Yet more and more he smiles upon | o | o | o | o |
| | The happy revolution. | o | x | o | x |
| | Why should we then suspect or fear | o | o | o | o |
| | The Influences of a year | o | x | x | o |
| | So smiles upon us the first morn, | o | o | x | o |
| | And speaks us good so soon as born? | o | o | o | o |
| | Pox on't! the last was ill enough, | o | o | o | o |
| | This cannot but make better proof; | o | x | o | o |
| | Or, at the worst, as we brush'd through | x | o | o | o |
| | The last, why so we may this too; | o | o | o | o |
| | And then the next in reason shou'd, | o | o | o | o |
| 38 | Be superexcellently good . . . | x | o | x | o |

For an English poet, Cotton is an uncommonly rich scudder and, in fact, outranks Marvell in the use of long words and rare modulations but also is much inferior to him artistically. He is the only poet among those I have studied whose iambic tetrameters contain a number of the unusual scud variation I+II, with or without tilt (e.g., *The Retreat*, l. 8, "And to my admiration finde"; *Valedictory*, l. 22, "Scarsely to Apprehension knowne"; *The Entertainment to Phillis*, l. 25, "Vessells of the true Antick mold"; and a few others).

viii. Matthew Prior (1664–1721), *An Epitaph* ("Interr'd beneath this Marble Stone"; pub. 1718):

| | | I | II | III | IV |
|---|---|---|---|---|---|
| 17 | Their Moral and Œconomy | o | x | o | x |
| | Most perfectly They made agree: | o | x | o | o |
| | Each Virtue kept it's proper Bound, | o | o | o | o |
| | Nor Trespass'd on the other's Ground. | o | x | o | o |
| | Nor Fame, nor Censure They regarded: | o | o | o | o |
| | They neither Punish'd, nor Rewarded. | o | o | o | o |
| | He car'd not what the Footmen did: | o | o | o | o |
| | Her Maids She neither prais'd, nor chid: | o | o | o | o |

| | | | | |
|---|---|---|---|---|
| o | o | o | o | So ev'ry Servant took his Course; |
| o | o | o | o | And bad at First, They all grew worse. |
| x | o | o | o | *Slothful* Disorder fill'd His Stable; |
| o | o | o | o | And sluttish Plenty deck'd Her Table. |
| o | o | o | o | Their Beer was strong; Their Wine was Port; |
| o | o | o | o | 30 Their Meal was large; Their Grace was short. |

I have chosen the most modulated passage in this poem by an essentially second-rate performer true to his pedestrian age. Another sequence of the same number of lines (37–50) is completely scudless. The occurrence of scuds—when they do appear—in II is characteristic of poorly modulated, commonplace poems in which the scudless type of line greatly predominates. The rarity of tilts (in accordance with contemporaneous theory) is also symptomatic of prosodic poverty in poems of that period.

IX. Jonathan Swift (1667–1745), *Stella's Birth-day* (1726–27):

| I | II | III | IV | |
|---|---|---|---|---|
| o | o | o | o | 1 This Day, whate'er the Fates decree, |
| o | o | o | o | Shall still be kept with Joy by me: |
| o | o | o | o | This Day then, let us not be told, |
| o | o | o | o | That you are sick, and I grown old, |
| o | o | o | o | Nor think on our approaching Ills, |
| o | o | x | o | And talk of Spectacles and Pills; |
| o | o | o | o | To morrow will be Time enough |
| o | o | x | o | To hear such mortifying Stuff. |
| o | o | o | o | Yet since from Reason may be brought |
| o | x | o | o | A better and more pleasing Thought, |
| o | o | o | o | Which can in spite of all Decays, |
| o | o | o | o | Support a few remaining Days: |
| x | o | x | o | From not the gravest of Divines, |
| o | o | o | o | 14 Accept for once some serious Lines. |

This jogging rhythm, with isolated, halfhearted scuds and an avoidance of tilts, is typical of the "light verse" (a ponderous and dreary machine) of the Age of Reason. Some may not think that l. 8 should be allowed a full scud in III. I am not quite sure I should have included Swift's doggerel.

x. John Dyer (1700?–58), *Grongar Hill* (pub. 1726):

| | I | II | III | IV |
|---|---|---|---|---|
| 79 And there the fox securely feeds; | o | o | o | o |
| And there the pois'nous adder breeds | o | o | o | o |
| Conceal'd in ruins, moss and weeds; | o | o | o | o |
| While, ever and anon, there falls | o | x | o | o |
| Huge heaps of hoary moulder'd walls. | o | o | o | o |
| Yet time has seen, that lifts the low, | o | o | o | o |
| And level lays the lofty brow, | o | o | o | o |
| Has been this broken pile compleat, | o | o | o | o |
| Big with the vanity of state; | x | o | x | o |
| But transient is the smile of fate! | o | o | o | o |
| A little rule, a little sway, | o | o | o | o |
| A sun beam in a winter's day, | o | x | o | o |
| Is all the proud and mighty have | o | o | o | o |
| 92 Between the cradle and the grave. | o | o | x | o |

A tame and typical minor poet endowed with a certain delicacy of touch and not as color-blind as most of his grove-and-rill brethren in that most inartistic of centuries.

xi. Samuel Johnson (1709–84), *On the Death of Dr. Robert Levet* (written 1782; pub. 1783):

| | I | II | III | IV |
|---|---|---|---|---|
| 1 Condemn'd to hope's delusive mine, | o | o | o | o |
| As on we toil from day to day, | o | o | o | o |
| By sudden blasts, or slow decline, | o | o | o | o |
| Our social comforts drop away. | o | o | o | o |
| Well tried through many a varying year, | o | o | o | o |
| See Levet to the grave descend; | o | x | o | o |
| Officious, innocent, sincere, | o | o | x | o |
| Of ev'ry friendless name the friend. | o | o | o | o |
| Yet still he fills affection's eye, | o | o | o | o |
| Obscurely wise, and coarsely kind; | o | o | o | o |
| Nor, letter'd arrogance, deny | o | o | x | o |
| Thy praise to merit unrefin'd. | o | o | x | o |
| When fainting nature call'd for aid, | o | o | o | o |
| 14 And hov'ring death prepar'd the blow ... | o | o | o | o |

The scant microbes of rhythm are a good test-tube sample of Samuel Johnson's plain rhythms.

XII. William Cowper (1731–1800), *Written after Leaving Her at New Burns* (written c. 1754; pub. 1825):

| I | II | III | IV | |
|---|----|-----|----|---|
| x | o | o | o | 12 *Welcome* my long-lost love, she said, |
| o | o | o | o | E'er since our adverse fates decreed |
| o | o | o | o | That we must part, and I must mourn |
| o | o | o | o | Till once more blest by thy return, |
| x | o | o | o | Love, on whose influence I relied |
| o | o | o | o | For all the transports I enjoy'd, |
| o | o | o | o | Has play'd the cruel tyrant's part, |
| o | o | x | o | And turn'd tormentor to my heart; |
| o | o | x | o | But let me hold thee to my breast, |
| o | x | o | o | Dear partner of my joy and rest, |
| o | o | o | o | And not a pain, and not a fear |
| o | o | o | o | Or anxious doubt, shall enter there.— |
| x | o | o | o | *Happy*, thought I, the favour'd youth, |
| x | x | o | o | 25 Blest with such undissembled truth! |

Cowper has left very few iambic tetrameters. Those of several of his flat *Olney Hymns* are not worth dissecting. The modulations of this poem come rather as a surprise (and perhaps reveal the concentrated music that the poor sick man had in him), seeing the pedestrian quality of most of his rhythms. I have chosen this passage to get in the very rare I + II.

XIII. William Wordsworth (1770–1850), *A Whirl-blast from Behind the Hill* (composed 1798; pub. 1800):

| I | II | III | IV | |
|---|----|-----|----|---|
| o | x | o | o | 1 A whirl-blast from behind the hill |
| o | o | o | o | Rushed o'er the wood with startling sound; |
| o | o | o | o | Then—all at once the air was still, |
| o | o | o | o | And showers of hailstones pattered round. |
| o | o | o | o | Where leafless oaks towered high above, |
| o | o | o | o | I sat within an undergrove |
| o | o | o | o | Of tallest hollies, tall and green; |
| o | o | o | o | A fairer bower was never seen. |
| o | o | o | o | From year to year the spacious floor |
| o | o | o | o | With withered leaves is covered o'er, |
| o | o | o | o | And all the year the bower is green. |
| o | o | o | o | But see! where'er the hailstones drop |

|                                               | I | II | III | IV |
|-----------------------------------------------|---|----|-----|----|
| The withered leaves all skip and hop;         | o | o  | o   | o  |
| 14 There's not a breeze—no breath of air . . . | o | o  | o   | o  |

The poem, which is an admirable one, seems to have been deliberately kept almost scudless by its author, save for a burst of music toward the end, with the final line (22) scudded on II and IV ("Were dancing to the minstrelsy"). Wordsworth's later tetrameters are also sparsely scudded, with singing lines here and there interrupting lengthy spells of regular ones. With the Hudibrastic nightmare hardly more than a century old, no wonder genuine poets were chary of their scuds in serious verse. That Wordsworth could orchestrate his scuds brilliantly is proved by such lines as 1342–45 of *The White Doe of Rylstone* (composed 1807–08; pub. 1815):

> Athwart the unresisting tide
> Of the spectators occupied
> In admiration or dismay,
> Bore instantly his Charge away

in which the combination of scuds (II, I+III, I+III, II) produces a very Pushkinian modulation. In the same poem occurs the very rare I+II line (754):

> With unparticipated gaze . . .

XIV. Samuel Taylor Coleridge (1772–1834), *The Pains of Sleep* (composed 1803; pub. 1816):

|                                               | I | II | III | IV |
|-----------------------------------------------|---|----|-----|----|
| 14 But yester-night I prayed aloud            | o | o  | o   | o  |
| In anguish and in agony,                      | o | x  | o   | x  |
| Up-starting from the fiendish crowd           | o | x  | o   | o  |
| Of shapes and thoughts that tortured me:      | o | o  | o   | o  |
| A lurid light, a trampling throng,            | o | o  | o   | o  |
| Sense of intolerable wrong,                   | x | o  | x   | o  |
| And whom I scorned, those only strong!        | o | o  | o   | o  |
| Thirst of revenge, the powerless will         | x | o  | o   | o  |
| Still baffled, and yet burning still!         | o | x  | o   | o  |
| Desire with loathing strangely mixed          | o | o  | o   | o  |
| On wild or hateful objects fixed.             | o | o  | o   | o  |

| | | | | |
|---|---|---|---|---|
| o | o | o | o | Fantastic passions! maddening brawl! |
| o | o | o | o | And shame and terror over all! |
| x | o | o | o | 27 Deeds to be hid that were not hid . . . |

In this great poem, contractions and split tilts add to the rippling of scuds, which here and there occur in consecutive lines as they do in the verses of Andrew Marvell and Matthew Arnold.

xv. George Gordon, Lord Byron (1788–1824), *Mazeppa* (composed 1818; pub. 1819):

| I | II | III | IV | |
|---|---|---|---|---|
| o | o | x | o | 15 Such was the hazard of the die; |
| o | o | o | o | The wounded Charles was taught to fly |
| o | o | o | o | By day and night through field and flood, |
| x | o | o | o | Stained with his own and subjects' blood; |
| o | o | o | o | For thousands fell that flight to aid: |
| x | o | o | o | And not a voice was heard to upbraid |
| o | x | o | o | Ambition in his humbled hour, |
| o | o | o | o | When Truth had nought to dread from Power. |
| o | o | o | o | His horse was slain, and Gieta gave |
| o | o | o | o | His own—and died the Russians' slave. |
| o | o | o | o | This, too, sinks after many a league |
| o | o | o | o | Of well-sustained, but vain fatigue; |
| x | o | o | o | And in the depths of forests darkling, |
| o | x | o | o | 28 The watch-fires in the distance sparkling . . . |

*Mazeppa* is not one of Byron's happiest compositions, but it serves my purpose as being mostly in iambic tetrameter. I have selected a passage from it to show his scudding at its poor best. The commonplace idiom is not redeemed, as it is in Wordsworth, by a concentration of rich poetical sense.

xvi. John Keats (1795–1821), *The Eve of St. Mark* (composed 1819):

| I | II | III | IV | |
|---|---|---|---|---|
| o | o | o | o | 1 Upon a Sabbath-day it fell; |
| o | o | o | o | Twice holy was the Sabbath-bell, |
| o | o | o | o | That call'd the folk to evening prayer; |
| o | o | o | o | The city streets were clean and fair |

| | I | II | III | IV |
|---|---|---|---|---|
| From wholesome drench of April rains; | o | o | o | o |
| And, on the western window panes, | x | o | o | o |
| The chilly sunset faintly told | o | o | o | o |
| Of unmatur'd green vallies cold, | x | o | o | o |
| Of the green thorny bloomless hedge, | x | o | o | o |
| Of rivers new with spring-tide sedge, | o | o | o | o |
| Of primroses by shelter'd rills, | o | x | o | o |
| And daisies on the aguish hills. | o | x | o | o |
| Twice holy was the Sabbath-bell: | o | o | o | o |
| 14  The silent streets were crowded well . . . | o | o | o | o |

The iambic tetrameter is not Keats' favorite medium of expression. He interrupts its flow either with shorter, lilted lines, as in *La Belle Dame Sans Merci* (in which each quatrain ends in a cadential line), or with sequences of trochaic tetrameters, as in the batch coming after l. 30 in *The Eve of St. Mark*. In the minds of many English poets of the time, tetrametrics were associated with folklore, naïve ditties, knights-errant, minstrelsy, fairy tales, and so forth.

XVII. Alfred, Lord Tennyson (1809–92), *In Memoriam*, XI (pub. 1850):

| | I | II | III | IV |
|---|---|---|---|---|
| 1  Calm is the morn without a sound, | o | o | o | o |
| Calm as to suit a calmer grief, | x | o | o | o |
| And only through the faded leaf | o | x | o | o |
| The chestnut pattering to the ground: | o | o | x | o |
| Calm and deep peace on this high wold, | x | o | o | o |
| And on these dews that drench the furze, | x | o | o | o |
| And all the silvery gossamers | o | o | o | x |
| That twinkle into green and gold; | o | o | o | o |
| Calm and still light on yon great plain | x | o | o | o |
| That sweeps with all its autumn bowers, | o | o | o | o |
| And crowded farms and lessening towers, | o | o | o | o |
| To mingle with the bounding main: | o | x | o | o |
| Calm and deep peace in this wide air, | x | o | o | o |
| 14    These leaves that redden to the fall . . . | o | o | x | o |

I have chosen this as a particularly brilliant example of scudding (based mainly on monosyllabics and partly owing to the repetition of a specific split tilt). There are, however, other sequences of fourteen or more lines in other parts of *In Memoriam* in which there are no scuds at all, or in which these are reduced to one half of their value (e.g., sec. XV). See also pp. 15–16.

XVIII. Robert Browning (1812–89), *Porphyria's Lover* (1836):

| I | II | III | IV | | |
|---|----|-----|-----|----|----|
| o | o | o | o | 29 | For love of her, and all in vain: |
| o | o | o | o | | So, she was come through wind and rain. |
| o | o | x | o | | Be sure I looked up at her eyes |
| x | o | o | o | | *Happy* and proud; at last I knew |
| o | o | o | o | | Porphyria worshipped me; surprise |
| o | o | o | o | | Made my heart swell, and still it grew |
| o | o | o | o | | While I debated what to do. |
| o | o | o | o | | That moment she was mine, mine, fair, |
| x | o | o | o | | *Perfectly* pure and good: I found |
| o | o | o | o | | A thing to do, and all her hair |
| o | o | o | o | | In one long yellow string I wound |
| o | o | o | o | | Three times her little throat around, |
| o | o | o | o | | And strangled her. No pain felt she; |
| o | o | o | o | 42 | I am quite sure she felt no pain. |

As already noted, the perception of semiscuds is a somewhat subjective affair and depends very much on the accentuation of adjacent words in the line. "She's," "me's," and "I's" may be sometimes very slightly accented, as I think they are here. Browning crams his iambic tetrameter so full of solid words that no wonder this admirable poem is so little scudded. There is a wonderful long tilt in l. 21, "Murmuring how she loved me— she," and the still more beautiful one in l. 37, which induced me to choose this passage. Split reverse tilts are also characteristic of his style.

XIX. Matthew Arnold (1822–88), *Resignation* (pub. 1849):

| I | II | III | IV | | |
|---|----|-----|-----|-----|----|
| o | o | o | o | 122 | Signs are not wanting, which might raise |
| o | o | o | o | | The ghosts in them of former days— |

| | | | | |
|---|---|---|---|---|
| Signs are not wanting, if they would; | o | o | x | o |
| Suggestions to disquietude. | o | x | o | x |
| For them, for all, time's busy touch, | o | o | o | o |
| While it mends little, troubles much. | o | o | o | o |
| Their joints grow stiffer—but the year | o | o | x | o |
| Runs his old round of dubious cheer; | o | o | o | o |
| *Chilly* they grow—yet winds in March | x | o | o | o |
| Still, sharp as ever, freeze and parch; | o | o | o | o |
| They must live still—and yet, God knows, | o | o | o | o |
| *Crowded* and keen the country grows; | x | o | o | o |
| It seems as if, in their decay, | o | o | o | o |
| 135 The law grew stronger every day. | o | o | o | o |

Further on, in l. 160, there occurs the rare long tilt ("Beautiful eyes meet his—and he"). Arnold's tetrameters are splendidly modulated and marked by that special device of artists in prosody, the interruption of musically flowing lines by compact verses full of false spondees. Compare all this with the snip-snap banalities of, say, Arthur Hugh Clough (1819–61), a poetaster, or the eighteenth-century meagerness of modulation in Byron's flat iambic tetrameters (e.g., *The Isles of Greece*, in which geographical names produce the few good scuds).

| | I | II | III | IV |
|---|---|---|---|---|
| xx. William Morris (1834–96), *Old Love* (pub. 1858): | | | | |
| 9 He gazed at the great fire a while: | o | x | o | o |
| "And you are getting old, Sir John;" | o | o | o | o |
| (He said this with that cunning smile | o | x | o | o |
| That was most sad;) "we both wear on, | o | o | o | o |
| Knights come to court and look at me, | o | o | o | o |
| With eyebrows up, except my lord, | o | o | o | o |
| And my dear lady, none I see | o | o | o | o |
| That know the ways of my old sword." | o | o | o | o |
| (My lady! at that word no pang | o | x | o | o |
| Stopp'd all my blood.) "But tell me, John, | o | o | o | o |
| Is it quite true that pagans hang | o | o | o | o |
| So thick about the east, that on | o | o | o | x |
| The eastern sea no Venice flag | o | o | o | o |
| 22 Can fly unpaid for?" "True," I said . . . | o | o | o | o |

This minor poet, a kind of sterile cross between the stylizations of Tennyson and those of Browning, is no "master of the iambic tetrameter" (as I think Saintsbury has termed him), but he has not unpleasingly experimented in subdued rhyme and curious run-on patterns. The enjambment from one quatrain to another via an unaccented monosyllabic rhyme word in l. 20 is a rarity. The postverbal "on" (closing 12) is of course accented in speech and is not a rare rhyme.

xxi. Modulations in *EO*, Four : ix, x, and xi:

| I | II | III | IV | | |
|---|----|-----|----|---|---|
| o | o | o | o | 1 | *Tak tóchno dúmal móy Evgéniy.* |
| o | o | x | o | | *On v pérvoy yúnosti svoéy* |
| o | o | x | o | | *Bïl zhértvoy búrnïh zabluzhdéniy* |
| x | o | x | o | | *I neobúzdannïh strastéy.* |
| o | o | x | o | | *Privíchkoy zhízni izbalóvan,* |
| o | o | x | o | | *Odním na vrémya ocharóvan,* |
| x | o | x | o | | *Razocharóvannïy drugím,* |
| o | o | x | o | | *Zhelán'em médlenno tomím,* |
| o | o | x | o | | *Tomím i vétrennïm uspéhom,* |
| o | o | x | o | | *Vnimáya v shúme i v tishí* |
| o | o | x | o | | *Roptán'e véchnoe dushí,* |
| o | x | o | o | | *Zevótu podavlyáya sméhom:* |
| o | o | o | o | | *Vot, kak ubíl on vósem' lét,* |
| o | o | o | o | 14 | *Utrátya zhízni lúchshiy tsvét.* |

| I | II | III | IV | | |
|---|----|-----|----|---|---|
| o | o | x | o | 1 | *V krasávits ón uzh ne vlyublyálsya,* |
| x | o | o | o | | *A volochílsya kák-nibúd';* |
| o | o | x | o | | *Otkázhut—mígom uteshálsya;* |
| o | o | x | o | | *Izményat—rád bïl otdohnút'.* |
| o | o | x | o | | *On íh iskál bez upoén'ya,* |
| x | o | x | o | | *A ostavlyál bez sozhalén'ya,* |
| o | o | o | o | | *Chut' pómnya íh lyubóv' i zlóst'.* |
| o | x | o | o | | *Tak tóchno ravnodúshnïy góst'* |
| o | o | x | o | | *Na víst vechérniy priezzháet,* |
| o | o | x | o | | *Sadítsya; kónchilas' igrá:* |
| x | o | x | o | | *On uezzháet so dvorá,* |

| | | I | II | III | IV |
|---|---|---|---|---|---|
| | *Spokóyno dóma zasïpáet,* | o | o | x | o |
| | *I sám ne znáet poutrú,* | o | o | x | o |
| 14 | *Kudá poédet vvecherú.* | o | o | x | o |

| | | I | II | III | IV |
|---|---|---|---|---|---|
| 1 | *No, poluchív poslán'e Táni,* | x | o | o | o |
| | *Onégin zhívo trónut bïl:* | o | o | o | o |
| | *Yazïk devícheskih mechtániy* | o | o | x | o |
| | *V nyom dúmï róem vozmutíl;* | o | o | x | o |
| | *I vspómnil ón Tat'yánï míloy* | o | o | o | o |
| | *I blédnïy tsvét, i víd untíloy;* | o | o | o | o |
| | *I v sládostnïy, bezgréshnïy són* | o | x | o | o |
| | *Dushóyu pogruzílsya ón.* | o | x | o | o |
| | *Bït' mózhet, chúvstviy pïl starínnoy* | o | o | o | o |
| | *Im na minútu ovladél;* | x | o | x | o |
| | *No obmanút' on ne hotél* | x | o | x | o |
| | *Dovérchivost' dushí nevínnoy.* | o | x | o | o |
| | *Tepér' mï v sád pereletím,* | o | o | x | o |
| 14 | *Gde vstrétilas' Tat'yána s ním.* | o | x | o | o |

## 10. COUNTS OF MODULATIONS IN "EUGENE ONEGIN"

Pushkin's pet line was the *chetïrestopnïy yamb*, the iambic tetrameter. It has been calculated that during a quarter of a century, from his Lyceum period—say, 1814 —to the end of his life, January, 1837, he composed in this measure some 21,600 lines, which amounts to more than half of his entire output in any kind of verse. His most prolific years in regard to poetry were 1814, 1821, 1824, 1826, 1828, and especially 1830 and 1833 (from above 2000 to above 3000 lines yearly); his most barren years in the same respect were 1834 and 1836, with the annual count sinking to about 280. His greatest year in the production of iambic tetrameters was 1828, with some 2350 lines, after which there is a decided decline (e.g., only thirty-five such lines in 1832). I have taken these figures, with slight alterations, from the *Metrical Guide to Pushkin's Poems* (*Metricheskiy spravochnik k stihotvoreniyam A. S. Pushkina*, 1934).

After having composed his long poem *Poltava* (in which, incidentally, such passages as ll. 295–305 and 401–14 form *EO* stanza sequences of rhyme but do not present separate entities of sense) in one fortnight (Oct. 3–16, 1829, in St. Petersburg) Pushkin seems to have experienced a certain revulsion toward his pet line, although *EO* was not yet completed. His remarkable piece *A Small House in Kolomna* (forty octaves in iambic pentameter, 1829–30) opens with the petulant statement:

> Of the four-foot iambus I've grown tired.
> In it writes everyone. To boys this plaything
> 'Tis high time to abandon . . .

However, he used it again for *The Bronze Horseman* (1833), the most mature of his tetrametric masterpieces.

In these notes on prosody, when illustrating such devices as scuds, tilts, false spondees, and so forth, I have discussed several aspects of the versification of *EO*. From the complete table of the scud modulations of *EO*, given for all 5523 lines, it will be seen that the predominant rhythm is Scud III (2603 lines). This is typical of the Russian iambic tetrameter in general. It will also be noted that the sum of all other scudded lines is about equal to the number of scudless lines (1515). Chapter One is unique in variety and richness of scudding. Two, Three, Four, and Five resemble each other in general modulation. Six, Seven, and Eight offer a certain drop in some of the categories.

There are six stanzas in *EO* with every line scudded (Two : IX, Lenski's soul; Three : VI, gossip about Tatiana and Onegin; Three : XX, Tatiana's confession to nurse; Three : XXIV, Tatiana defended; Six : XIII, Lenski goes to visit Olga before duel; Six : XL, Lenski's tomb) and twenty-six stanzas with only one scudless line in each. No stanza is entirely scudless. The maximum amount of scudded lines is twenty-three in a row, and there are three cases of such sequences: Three : V : 11 to VII : 5; Three : XXIII : 11 to XXV : 5; and Six : XII : 6 to XIII : 14. In all these cases the vivid sustained melody coincides with a torrent of inspired eloquence.

A closer look at the six varieties of modulation (and here the bilingual reader should consult the original text of *EO*) reveals the following facts:

The maximum of first-foot scudders for any given stanza is four (in the last eight lines of One : XXXIII, the famous evocation of the amorous surf; and in Eight : XXIII, Onegin's second conversation with Princess N., "this painful tête-à-tête") and five (in the first seven lines of Six : X, Onegin's dissatisfaction with himself before the duel). In Chapter Seven (in which the number of first-foot scudders ebbs almost to one half of that found in Chapter One) we find runs of six and five stanzas completely deficient in this scud (VII–XIV, Olga's marriage and Tatiana's solitude; XXVIII–XXXII, departure; XLIII–XLVII, first impressions in Moscow).

The number of second-foot scudders, so abundant (100) in Chapter One, dwindles by almost one half in the last three chapters, in which there are also long runs of omissions (172 lines in a row in Eight, interrupted only by a single such scud in "Onegin's Letter"). There are several stanzas containing as many as five such scuds; and one stanza (One : XXI, Onegin's arrival at the theater) breaks the record with six. There are some interesting runs of consecutive second-foot scudders; e.g., four at the end of One : XXXII (see n. to One : XXXII : 11–14) and four at the end of Four : XLVI.

The commonest line in Russian poetry, the pastime of the cruising genius and the last refuge of the poetaster, is that facile and dangerous thing, the third-foot scudder.

It is the predominant melody in *EO* and is generally tri-partite; i.e., made up of three words or three logical units. The line "sings" (and may lull the Russian versificator into a state of false poetical security), especially in the frequent cases in which the central word in the third-foot scudded line has at least four syllables after a first word of two syllables, or has at least three syllables after an initial trisyllable. No stanza in *EO* consists exclusively of third-foot scudders; the closest approach to this is presented by Five : XXXV (end of name-day feast), with twelve such lines, and Six : XL (Lenski's tomb), with thirteen such lines. Sustained runs of this rhythm are often associated with a technique much favored by Pushkin, the rapid listing of various objects or actions.

The combination of two scuds in one verse, the fast first-foot scud and the flowing third-foot scud, is what gives vigor and brilliancy to a Russian poet's work, and Pushkin is a great artist in the use of this "fast flow." It is especially attractive when the line is followed or preceded by a second-foot scudder (see n. to One : XXIII : 11–13). The pleasure derived from the fast flow is owing not only to its euphony but also to the perception of its plenitude, of its perfect fit in regard to form and contents. The highest frequency of this line in any stanza is six (*Journey*, XXVIII). There are three stanzas with five such lines (Two : XI, Eugene's neighbors; Four : XXX, modish albums; and Eight : IX, defense of Onegin) and fifteen stanzas with four. Very sonorous and delightful are the runs of three consecutive fast flows in Four : XX : 9–11 (on relatives) and Six : XXVII : 3–5 (Onegin's retort to Zaretski).

The frequency of the "slow-flow" line (second-and-third-foot scudder) reaches the extraordinary figure of nine in the brilliantly scudded first chapter, in which it even occurs adjacently (see n. to One : LIII : 1–7). The decrease of II+III in all the other chapters may be the

result of Pushkin's deliberate control in regard to a
rococo rhythm.

I find the maximum number of scudless lines in a
stanza to be nine, and of such there are only two cases:
Three : II (Lenski and Onegin talk) and Six : XLIV (sober
maturity). In regard to runs of scudless lines (often associated with didactic or conversational passages), I find
nine stanzas having four such lines in a row, and five
stanzas having five in a row. The record is six consecutive nonscudders: Three : XXI : 5–8 (Tatiana speaking to
nurse) and Six : XXI : 4–9 (Lenski's lusterless elegy).

My list of scudded monosyllables commonly occurring
in *EO* comprises some forty words. Their bulk is made
up mainly of prepositions: *bez* ("without"), *chrez*
("through," "across"), *dlya* ("for"), *do* ("up to"), *iz*
("out"), *ko* ("to"), *mezh* ("between"), *na* ("on"), *nad*
("above"), *o* or *ob* ("about"), *ot* ("from"), *po* ("upon,"
"along"), *pod* ("under"), *pred* ("before"), *pri* ("by"),
*pro* ("about"), *skvoz'* ("through"), *so* ("with"), *sred'*
("amid"), *u* ("at"), *vo* ("in"), and *za* ("behind"). Next
come the conjunctions: *i* ("and"), *a* ("but," "and"), *da*
("and," "yet"), *no* ("but"), *il'* ("or"), *ni* ("nor"), *to*
("now," "then"), *chem* ("than"), *chto* ("that"), *chtob*
("in order to"), and *hot'* ("though"). Incidentally, the
scuddability of the last word is nicely proved by its vowel
being pronounced in good Russian as an unaccented *o*.
Finally, there are a few adverbs: *ne* ("not"), *kak* ("as,"
"like"), *uzh* ("already"), and the terminal particles,
conditional, interrogative, and emphatic: *bï*, *li*, and *zhe*.

The disyllables and the one staple trisyllable scudded
in *EO* have already been discussed under §4, Tilted
Scuds. They are: *pered*, *predo*, *peredo* ("before"), *oto*
("from"), *mezhdu* ("between"), *ili* ("or"), *chtobï* ("in
order to"), and *dabï* ("so as to"), all of them accented on
the first syllable in speech.

I have ignored the semiscuds completely (counting

them as regular beats) so as to avoid subjective prefer-
ences of intonation in assessing borderline cases. Their
number is negligible; but in order that other workers
may check my calculations when comparing their figures
with mine, something about such weak words, which are
not quite weak enough to be counted as scuds, should be
said. There is, first of all, *bït'* ("to be"), *bud'* ("be"), *bïl*
("was"), which I have invariably counted as beats, even
in such combinations as *chto-nibud'* ("something") and
*mozhet bït'* ("maybe"), which are generally accented as
dactyls in speech but not infrequently terminate a verse
with a masculine rhyme. Monosyllabic numerals (such
as *raz, dva, tri*, etc.), personal pronouns (*ya, tï, on*, etc.),
and possessive pronouns (*moy, tvoy*, etc.) can be very
weak semiscuds, especially in such dactylic locutions as
*bozhe moy* ("my goodness") or in the recurrent combination *moy Onegin. Chto* in the sense of "what," and
*kak* in the sense of "how," are almost good beats, and so
are *kto* ("who"), *tak* ("so"), *tam* ("there"), *tut* ("here"),
*gde* ("where"), *vot* ("now," "here"), and *sey* ("this").
The trickiest is the little group *bliz* ("near"), *vdal'*
("afar"), *vdol'* ("along"), *vkrug* ("around"), *vne* ("outside"), *chut'* ("barely"), and *lish'* ("only"), but I have
not succumbed to the temptation of having them influence my count. It is a curious thing that their allies
*skvoz'* and *chrez* are felt by Russian prosodists to be true
scuds (among which I place them), their pronunciation
being affected by the very transiency they help to express. Finally, there is *vsyo* ("all"), which I have left
among the semiscuds, although it is very weak when
spoken, especially in such anapaestic combinations as
*vsyo ravnó* ("all the same"). And among the disyllables
that produce a semiscudding effect (as examined in
another section) there are several pronouns, such as *oná*
("she"), *eyó* ("her," "hers"), *náshi* ("our," pl.), and to
these may be added the words *sredí* ("amid"), *hotyá*

("although"), *uzhé* ("already"), *kogdá* ("when"), *eshch-yó* ("still"), all of which slightly weaken the beat of the foot, especially when recurring in the beginning of several adjacent lines. None of these semiscuds have I taken into account when calculating the modulations in *EO*.

Consultation of the appended table may be facilitated by reference to the following examples of *EO* lines (the English versions faithfully follow the rhythm; the reader is reminded that a scud is an unaccented syllable coinciding with the stress of a metrical foot):

I: A line scudded on the first foot, or Fast:

> *I vozbuzhdát' ulíbku dám . . .*
> and to provoke the ladies' smiles . . .

II: A line scudded on the second foot, or Slow:

> *Sred' módnïh i starínnïh zál . . .*
> in modern and in ancient halls . . .

III: A line scudded on the third foot, or Flow:

> *Zarétski, nékogda buyán . . .*
> Zaretski, formerly a rough . . .

I + III: A line scudded on first and third feet, or Fast Flow:

> *V filosofícheskoy pustíne . . .*
> in philosophical reclusion . . .

II + III: A line scudded on second and third feet, or Slow Flow:

> *Blistátel'na, poluvozdúshna . . .*
> irradiant, half-insubstantial . . .

0: A scudless line, or Regular:

> *Porá nadézhd i grústi nézhnoy . . .*
> the time of hopes and tender sadness . . .

SCUD MODULATIONS IN "EO"

| CHAPTER | STAN-ZAS | I | II | III | I+ III | II+ III | O | TOTAL LINES |
|---|---|---|---|---|---|---|---|---|
| One | 54 | 58 | 100 | 306 | 74 | 9 | 209 | 756 |
| Two | 40 | 32 | 62 | 261 | 56 | — | 137 | 548 |
| Three | 41 | 33 | 50 | 268 | 58 | 2 | 157 | 568 |
| Four | 43 | 38 | 67 | 278 | 53 | 1 | 164 | 601 |
| Five | 42 | 41 | 66 | 282 | 39 | 2 | 158 | 588 |
| Six | 43 | 59 | 43 | 301 | 39 | 2 | 158 | 602 |
| Seven | 52 | 32 | 52 | 378 | 68 | 3 | 195 | 728 |
| Eight | 51 | 50 | 41 | 325 | 76 | 1 | 205 | 698 |
| Prefatory Piece | — | 3 | 7 | 2 | — | 5 | | 17 |
| T.'s Letter in Three | | 8 | 6 | 31 | 6 | — | 28 | 79 |
| O.'s Letter in Eight | | 8 | 1 | 26 | 1 | — | 24 | 60 |
| Added in n. to Six | | — | 1 | 11 | 1 | — | 1 | 14 |
| Added in n. to Eight | | — | 1 | 2 | — | — | 2 | 5 |
| O.'s Journey | | 15 | 15 | 127 | 29 | 1 | 72 | 259 |
| Totals | | 374 | 508 | 2603 | 502 | 21 | 1515 | 5523 |

## 11. OTHER METERS AND RHYTHMS

These notes on prosody, meant only to give the reader a clear idea of the meter used by Pushkin in *EO*, cannot include a study of other metrical forms, beyond the remarks made on their origination. Suffice it to add that the similarities and distinctions between Russian and English forms remain the same throughout. What has been said of scud, tilt, elision, and contraction in special reference to the iambic tetrameter is also applicable of course to its trochaic counterpart and to the other lengths of binaries in use, such as trimeters and pentameters. In ternaries, scudding is possible too, but is of an extremely infrequent occurrence (being even rarer in English than in Russian), whereas the tilts possible in ternary lines belong to another type than those occurring in duplex feet, since in triplex ones they do not involve the stress but coincide with two adjacent depressions.

Iambic trimeters, those chimes of pocket poetry, whose lilting rhythm in English affords an easy line of communication between meter and cadence, have not thrived in Russian: I can recall no serious first-rate piece composed entirely in that measure. Tyutchev's famous stanzas beginning:

> *Zimá nedárom zlítsya,*
> *Proshlá eyó porá . . .*
>
> No wonder winter glowers,
> His season has gone by . . .

belong definitely to the lightweight category.

The iambic pentameter, rhymed or unrhymed, is not so abundantly represented in Russian as it is in English, but its blank-verse form vies with its English and German models in monosyllabic tilts, enjambments, and shifts of caesura (see especially Pushkin's "diminutive dramas"), while a greater variety of scuds and the free admission of sonorous feminine terminations among crisp masculine ones go far to compensate for the absence of elision and disyllabic tilting.

The iambic hexameter, which can breathe freely only if the modulations of long scuddable words lend sinuosity to its hemistichs, withers in English, being choked by fill-up words, dull masculine rhymes, and gritty monosyllables; but in Russian poetry it becomes an extremely musical meander because of fluid scuds and the melody of true cross rhyme (feminines interlaced with masculines). It should be noted that the Russian iambic hexameter permits a scudded caesura, which is taboo in its model, the French Alexandrine. Here is an example of what a Russian elegiac stanza would sound like if transposed into English iambic hexameters:

> A linden avenue where light and shadow mingle
> Leads to an ancient slab of opalescent stone,
> Whereon the visitor distinguishes a single
> Unperishable word to scholarship unknown.

Trochaic tetrameters are considerably more seldom used for serious verse than iambic ones in Russian but have provided a form for several memorable poems (such as Pushkin's *Fairy Tales*). Their system of scuds is exactly similar to that of the iambic tetrameter. It should be marked that in a tetrametric piece iambic lines are never combined with trochaic ones, as they have been by several English experimentators (Milton, Blake, Coleridge). On the other hand, a form that is very rare in English poetry—namely, the trochaic pentameter (used, for instance, by Browning in *One Word More*, 1855)—was established by Trediakovski in an idyl of 1752 and has provided Lermontov, Blok, and others with a remarkably musical medium of expression, which I can only mimic here:

> Nobody has managed to unravel
> That inscription on the stone; and yet
> Fools get formidable grants to travel
> To the limits of their alphabet.

Ternary meters have thrived in Russia. Owing to the facility with which a Russian rhymester can launch a line upon a dactyl, Russian dactylic hexameters are not so repulsive as English ones, and ternary trimeters are among the most harmonious forms extant. The amphibrachic trimeter in English is generally intermixed with anapaestic lines. The purest example is probably Swinburne's, otherwise dreadful, *Dolores* (1866).

Scuds and tilts occur also in ternary feet, but the situation is somewhat different from that obtained in binaries.

Scudded feet in ternaries are comparatively rare; here

are some examples of such modulations in (1) anapaestic, (2) amphibrachic, and (3) dactylic trimeters scudded on the second foot:

(1) None too prosperous but not a pauper
*Nezazhitochnïy, no i ne nishchiy*

(2) Lived opulently but not wisely
*Roskoshestvoval, no ne mudro*

(3) Sorrowful but not submissive
*Gorestnïy, no ne pokornïy*

Incidentally, as every poet knows, (1) can be also scanned as a trochaic pentameter (with a scud on "-rous" and a semiscud on both "None" and "not"); (2), as an iambic tetrameter (with two adjacent scuds in II and III, "-lent" and "but"); and (3), as a trochaic tetrameter (with scuds also in II and III, "-ful" and "not").

Disyllabic tilts in ternaries are not associated with scuds (as they are in binaries), since, as already mentioned, they coincide with two adjacent depressions. The disyllable is practically neutralized into a pyrrhic. Their occurrence is common. An obvious example in Russian is the third verse of Zemfira's song in Pushkin's *The Gypsies* (composed 1824):

*Starïy muzh, groznïy muzh . . .*
Husband old, husband fierce . . .

For an English example we may select the word "only" in an amphibrachic line (12) of Wordsworth's *The Reverie of Poor Susan* (composed 1797; pub. 1800):

The one only dwelling on earth that she loves.
*Odno tol'ko v mire ey lyubo zhil'yo.*

## 12. DIFFERENCES IN USE OF METER

In both English and Russian there is a definite predominance of binaries over ternaries; but this predominance
is perhaps more marked in English than in Russian. For
reasons basically associated with the brevity of English
words, an English poem in ternaries seems more diffuse,
more self-conscious, more dependent on artificial gap
filling, and, in fact, more difficult for the reader to tackle
than a poem in binary meter. There is no such effort
attending the assimilation of ternaries in Russian, in
which long words are frequent and in which, in consequence, a greater number of memorable dactyls,
anapaests, and amphibrachs than those in English have
been produced.

Pausative forms (connecting meter and cadence) came
naturally to English poets since ancient time and did a
great deal to alleviate both the monotony and the orna-
mentality of English ternary feet. In Russian, omissions
of depressions, resulting in pausative verse, did not come
into general use until Blok (by far the greatest poet of
the first two decades of this century), borrowing the device from German cadence (rather than from English
cadence), composed a number of magnificent short
poems in it. But Tyutchev, as early as 1832 (in the
poem *Silentium*, first published that year in *Molva*),
had already inaugurated the musical gasp of mixed or
broken meter, which he followed up by his Heinian *Last
Love*, first published in 1854 (*Sovremennik*). Cadential
forms might have been evolved directly out of syllabic
ones in Russia if a poet of genius had thought of it before
Lomonosov introduced metrical prosody. Derzhavin did
leave some experimental verse in that direction, but the
rigid adherence of the Zhukovski-Batyushkov-Pushkin
school to regular meter in serious poetry precluded the
acceptance of cadential lilts.

English poets, when they do turn to ternions, so consistently and so naturally intermingle anapaestic lines with amphibrachic ones that the English student of verse, unacquainted with other languages, is apt to dismiss the amphibrach altogether as an arbitrary meter devised by the ingenuity of prosodists (along with the molossus and what not)* and to regard the amphibrachic lines, even when they predominate in a poem, as acephalous anapaests. In Russian, on the other hand, until the emancipation of meter associated with Blok's name, there was a definite tendency on the part of poets using ternaries to have every line of the poem, no matter how long (except for imitations of the so-called classical hexameters, in which omissions of depressions were permitted), run strictly amphibrachically, or strictly anapaestically, or strictly dactylically.

The most striking difference between Russian and English poems in binaries is the application to English iambics of the device of decapitation (which the anapaest, being bicephalous, can after all survive). The introduction of random trochaic tetrameters, or sequences of them, starting and affirming themselves as iambic tetrameters, is so usual with English poets, and has assisted them in producing such enchanting pieces, that in the light of these examples the trochee is demoted by the theorist to the rank of acephalous iamb. The interruption of an iambic sequence of lines by a trochaic line or lines is completely alien to Russian prosody, as studied in retrospect, but there is no particular reason why such variations could not be introduced. However, an organic reason for their absence may be traced to the general difference between Russian and English, a difference reflected both in speech and in metrical composition. This

---

*While perversely retaining the spondee and the pyrrhic, which are *not* feet, since no poem, not even a couplet, can be wholly made up of them in terms of metrical prosody.

difference is the greater rigidity, strength, and clarity of the single accent in a Russian word of any length, which leads to a sharper shock in the unexpected passage from an iambic line to a trochaic one (the looser and duller modulations of ternaries in Russian allow the passage from one ternary meter to another much more easily). In an English long word, on the other hand, a secondary accent often takes some of the burden of emphasis off the back of the main accented syllable; and in English verse, the existence of duplex tilt and scudded rhyme (both of which occur only in a rudimentary form in Russian poetry) illustrate the English elasticity of meter, of which, in tetrameters, the trochaic line takes such delightful advantage in rippling the couplet that had been ostentatiously begun by an iambic smoothness of sound in the preceding verse.

13. RHYME

If we exclude a few scattered masterpieces (such as Pushkin's beautiful but obviously derivative dramas), we can say that the medium of blank verse has not produced in Russia, during the two hundred years of its metrical history, anything similar in scope, splendor, and universal influence to the unrhymed iambic pentameter in England since Chaucer's day. On the other hand, there has not appeared, in the course of half a millennium, a rhymed English romance in iambic tetrameter comparable in artistic merit to Pushkin's *Eugene Onegin*. Further on, to simplify the comparison, the discussion of Russian and English rhymes is limited to nineteenth-century practice.

Rhyme is not a component of meter, not part of the final foot, but rather its stub or its shoe, or its spur. It may closely fit the ultima when it coincides with the last ictus in masculine lines (hence masculine rhymes or masculines, stressed on the only, or last, syllable of a word) or else it may be an ornamental and (in French and Russian) very beautiful appendage of feminine lines or of long lines (hence feminine rhymes or feminines, stressed on the penultimate, and long rhymes, stressed on the antepenultimate). The terms "single," "double," and "triple" used by some English theorists for masculine, feminine, and long are ambiguous because rhyme is not the participating word but the effect of two, three, or more "like endings" (to use a famous definition of rhyme); therefore, a "single rhyme" would correctly mean one set of such endings in a piece of verse (e.g., "like endings" throughout a poem). What I term the "long rhyme" Russian theorists call a "dactylic rhyme," which is extremely misleading not only because rhyme lies outside meter and should not be expressed in metrical terms, but also because a long rhyme, or long terminal, when attached to a line of binary verse, does not sound at all like the dactylic chime of the long rhyme, or long terminal, in ternary verse. In the case of iambics or trochees, the ear distinguishes an extrametrical echo of the binary measure, and the voice (while not giving the ultima the kind of value it gives a scudded masculine) reads the final, unaccented syllable more abruptly than it would the same syllable, had ternaries been scanned.

A further removal proximad of the accent results in stunt rhyme, which has not yet been instrumental in producing any major poetry either in English or in Russian. It should be noted that the feminine rhyme and the longer variants may involve two or more words.

Rhyme may be adjacent (in couplets, triplets, etc.) or alternate (bcbc, bcbcbc, abab, baba, AbAb, etc.)* or in-

*Here and elsewhere vowels denote feminines, consonants denote masculines, and capital vowels denote long rhymes.

closing (one rhyme inclosing or "embracing" a couplet or a triplet; e.g., abba, bcccb, etc.).

The more distant a rhyme word is from its fellow in level of sense or grammatical category, the "richer" the rhyme is felt to be.

A rhyme may be formed by terminals spelled differently, such as "laugh–calf," "tant–temps," *lyod–kot* (Russian for "ice–cat"), which are then termed ear rhymes.

Eye rhymes, no longer used in French ("aimer–mer"), are permissible by tradition in English ("grove–love")\* and are barely possible in Russian, as in the case of *rog–Bog* ("horn–God"), the latter being pronounced generally "boh," with *h* as in "hob"; or *vóronï–stóronï* ("ravens–sides"), in which the second *o* in the second word is slurred so as almost, but not quite, to make the word sound disyllabic—a very rare case in Russian, in which, as a rule, the ear hears what the eye sees.† Perhaps the nearest approach to the English gynandrous type of rhyme, "flower–our," would be *storozh–morzh* ("watchman–walrus"), but I do not think that this has ever been tried.

Strictly speaking, there are no laws or rules of rhyme except the very general rule that a rhyme should afford at the best "satisfaction and surprise" (as the French say) or at least a sense of euphoric security (which goes for the routine rhyme in all languages), with a hereditary acceptance of certain conventions. But even these sensations can be altered and these traditions broken by any poet whose genius proves powerful and original enough to inaugurate imitable trends.

---

\*In English, such inexact rhymes as "love–off" or "grove–enough" rather curiously combine visual and auditory satisfaction or pain.

†It should be noted, however, that to elide *storoni* to make it a trochee in a binary line would be considered in even worse taste than to rhyme it with *voroni*.

The general difference between English and Russian rhyme is that there are considerably more feminine rhymes in Russian and that in diversity and richness the Russian rhyme is akin to the French rhyme. In result, Russian and French poets can afford the luxury of demanding more from the rhyme than English poets can afford to do. There is a certain subdued and delicate beauty of gray, gentle rhyme in English that is not duplicated in the dazzlingly brilliant romantic and neo-romantic arrays of French and Russian poets.

In French, the presence of at least two different consonants before a final *e muet* gives the latter a semblance of voice (*maître*, *lettre*, *nombre*, *chambre*, etc.) and allows the French poet to mimic both the meter and the feminine rhyme of English and Russian verse. If we devise the line:

> Le maître siffle, son chien tremble

it may be scanned (if we do so with more deliberation than a Frenchman would) not much differently from, say:

> The master whistles, his dog trembles

or from its Russian counterpart (in which, incidentally, the split reverse tilt is eliminated, together with the weak monosyllables):

> *Hozyáin svíshchet, pyós trepéshchet.*

Similarly, if we take the words:

> Phèdre (Fr.)
> feather (Eng.)
> *Fedra* (Russ.)

we may say that roughly they rhyme and that "Phèdre–cèdre" is as fully a feminine rhyme as "feather–weather" or "waiter–*véter*" (Russ. "wind"). A closer inspection, however, reveals that "Phèdre" is somewhat shorter, and "feather" (or "waiter") just a trifle shorter, than *Fedra* (or *véter*). This difference becomes immediately apparent if we take another set:

> mettre (Fr.)
> better (Eng.)
> *metr* (Russ. "meter,"
>     the measure of length)

*Metr–vetr* (archaic *veter*) is a masculine rhyme, but it is almost identical in terminal sound to the French "mettre" or "mètre." On the other hand, if an Englishman manages to pronounce *metr* correctly, it will form a gynandrous association with "better" only insofar as "fire" does with "higher."

Another type of *e muet* affecting the eye is what might be termed the deaf-mute *e*. If we take the words:

> palette (Fr.)
> let (Eng.)
> *let* (Russ. "of years")

it will be seen that what in French makes a feminine rhyme ("palette–omelette") is to the English and Russian ear a harmony with masculine endings in "-et." Consequently, if we devise the line:

> Telle montagne, telle aurore

it comes to the metrist as something of a shock that it is syllabically identical to the iambically sounding:

> Le maître siffle, son chien tremble.

We are now in a position to draw a comparison between English and Russian rhyme:

There are poems in Russian that consist of only masculine rhymes or only feminine rhymes, but whereas in English a feminine rhyme may crop up at random among a long sequence of masculines, no such cases occur in serious Russian verse. Neither in English nor in Russian is it necessary for a rigid scheme of rhyme to be sustained throughout a poem, but in a Russian freely rhymed poem, in which both kinds of rhymes occur, terminals belonging to different sets of rhymes will not be placed in adjacent lines (say, ababaececded, etc.) unless a certain standard scheme is deliberately repeated over and over again.

The Russian masculine rhyme allows identity to be limited to a final vowel if the latter is preceded by a vowel or a soft sign (*moyá*, "my," fem.; *tayá*, "concealing"; *ch'ya*, "whose," fem.); otherwise, it demands at least a two-letter coincidence (*moy*, "my," masc., and *Tolstóy*, or *son*, "dream," and *balkón*, "balcony") and it conforms to the rule of the *consonne d'appui* ("supporting consonant") whenever a consonant precedes the final vowel. *Da* ("yes") rhymes with *vodá* ("water") but not with *Moskvá*; and *tri* ("three") rhymes with *darí* ("give") and *utrí* ("wipe") but not with *prosí* ("ask") as "tree" and "see" would in English. In this respect a certain freedom is traditionally granted—owing to obvious lyrical reasons—to case endings of *lyubóv'*: *lyubví* ("of love") is allowed to rhyme with words in which the penult is a vowel; e.g., *tvoí* ("thy," pl.). Pushkin happens to go further: in Three : xiv, he rhymes *lyubví–dní* ("days"), which is not admissible and constitutes the one really bad rhyme in the whole of *EO*. In English it is, of course, the other way round, and although the support of a consonant is sometimes unavoidable—given the paucity of rhyme in general—such coincidences of sound as "sea–foresee" or "Peter–repeater" have been distasteful to most poets of the past.

A curious characteristic of Russian feminine rhymes is the license accorded to certain common unaccented endings. Let us consider the words

$$záli \text{ ("halls")}$$

>  *máliy* ("small")
>  *áloy* ("of the red," fem. gen.)
>  *zhálo* ("sting")
>  *Urála* ("of the Ural")

The endings after the *l* are all slightly different in sound, but a Russian poet of Pushkin's time and later will think nothing of rhyming *zalï–malïy*, *malïy–aloy*, and *zhalo–Urala*. Of these three types, the first is not inelegant; the second is absolutely correct (indeed, in old-fashioned or declamatory style the adjectival ending *ïy* is actually pronounced as an unaccented *oy*), and *zhalo–Urala*, though shocking to the purist, is frequently used (Pushkin rhymes both *rana*, "wound," and *rano*, "early," with "Tatiana"). *Zalï*, on the other hand, does not rhyme with *aloy* or *zhalo* or *Urala*, and the last does not rhyme with any of the first three in the column. There is no analogy for this in French, and only a very distant one in English (cf. "alley" and "rally" or such cockney assonances as "waiter–potato").

The feminine rhyme in Russian, as already mentioned, sounds a jot fuller and more fluent to the ear than the feminine rhyme in English. It is also (as well as the masculine) more of a masquerader than its English counterpart. The further proximad identity of spelling is carried, the more striking and more delightful the rhyme is deemed, granted that in the course of this improving consonance difference of sense grows in inverse ratio to that of sound. Thus, the identical rhyme *supruga* ("wife") and *supruga* (sing. gen. of *suprug*, "husband"), while conforming to the wonderful comical tone of the narrative poem wherein it occurs (Pushkin's *Graf Nulin*, 1825), would be weak in a serious piece.

In feminine rhymes or in two-letter masculine endings the *consonne d'appui* is welcome but not obligatory. Examples of rhymes that are rich owing to its presence and to other reasons are:

*sklon* ("slope")
*Apollón*

*prostóy* ("simple")
*zolotóy* ("golden")

*prostóy*
*Tolstóy*

*prostáya* (fem.)
*zolotáya* (fem.)

*prostáya*
*stáya* ("a flock")

*vstrecháet* ("meets")
*otvecháet* ("answers")

Richness of rhyme can also be achieved by such subtle shuttles of critical consonants as in *balkón–sklon*, in which ornamental support is provided by alliteration.

The existence of a scudded terminal in binary meters depends on the line's ending in a word of at least three syllables with a secondary accent either upon the ultima or on the antepenult; and since organically a Russian word can have but one accent, it follows that scudded rhyme (Scud IV in iambic tetrameter) does not occur in Russian poetry. A few cases occur as prosodic mistakes in old doggerels going back as far as the eighteenth century, and a few experiments by genuine poets have been made in our time. In 1918, during the Civil War, I remember Maksimilian Voloshin, an excellent and erudite poet (1877–1932), reading to me at a Yalta café, one cold and gloomy night with the sea booming and splashing over the parapet onto the pavement, a fine patriotic poem in which the pronoun *moya* or *tvoya* rhymed with the end of the line *i nepreodolimaya* ("and [tum-tee-]unsurmountable"), producing a I + II + IV scud combination.

The English situation is quite different. If we choose the word "solitude" for the ending of a line, we observe that a normal secondary accent on the ultima (especially conspicuous in American speech) affords a perch for a perfectly banal rhyme (say, "solitude–rude"). Not all long words, though, provide this support or, if they do, do so under coercion (e.g., "horrible" forced into rhyme with "dull" or "dell"). In other cases, tradition comes into play, and by an ancient rule of the poetical game or prosodical agreement, polysyllables ending in *y* ("-ty," "-ry," "-ny," etc.) may yield a dubious solace to the English versifier by rhyming with "see," "me," "tree," etc.

In Russian verse I find something faintly resembling a Semiscud IV only in the following case, which needs a brief preface. The Russian locution rendering the idea of "some" in relation to time, place, person, thing, or manner (sometime, somewhere, someone, something, somehow, etc.) is *-nibúd'*, and when properly printed is connected by a hyphen with the words for "when" (*kogda*), "where" (*gde*), "who" (*kto*), "what" (*chto*), "how" (*kak*), etc. Thus, *kogda-nibud'* means "sometime" or "someday," *gde-nibud'* means "somewhere," *kto-nibud'* means "someone" or "somebody," *chto-nibud'* means "something," *kak-nibud'* means "somehow," etc. Now, the point is that in ordinary speech, or in any part of a metrical line other than its terminal in binary verse, these compounds are accented on the syllable preceding the neutralized *-nibud'*. A line going:

> *Któ-nibud', któ-nibud', któ-nibud'*
> Somebody, somebody, somebody

is a regular dactylic trimeter with a long terminal. Moreover, a few of these forms, when inflected—e.g., *kakáya-nibud'* ("some kind of," fem.)—automatically receive a single accent on the first part of the compound and lack all accent on the end of the second part when participating in a binary line in which otherwise they could not find a scannable place.

Pushkin and other poets of his time rhyme *kto-nibud'*, *gde-nibud'*, etc., with *grud'* ("breast"), *put'* ("way"), *blesnút'* ("to flash"), etc. In describing Onegin's desultory and haphazard education, our poet starts a famous stanza (One : v) with the lines:

> Mï vsé uchílis' ponemnógu,
> Chemú-nibud' i kák-nibúd':
> Tak vospitán'em, sláva Bógu,
> U nás nemudrenó blesnút'.

> All of us had a bit of schooling
> in something and [tum-te-]somehow:
> therefore with culture, God be lauded,
> with us it is not hard to shine.

*Chemu-nibud'* is the dative of *chto-nibud'*, and the second line, in which it occurs:

> Chemu-nibud' i kak-nibud'
> ◡ ́ ◡ – ◡ ́ ◡ ̄

is modulated very much like

> With Cherubim and Seraphim

(Christina Rossetti, *The Convent Threshold*, l. 24). However, the Russian reader so little expects a scud on the final ictus that in reading Pushkin's line he would accent the *bud'* more than in ordinary speech.

In the first third of the nineteenth century in Russia there is a tendency on the part of good poets to resist the facile rhyme depending on verb endings (infinitives in *-at'*, *-et'*, *-it'*, *-ut'*; past tenses in *-al*, *-ala*, *-alo*, *-ali*, *-il*, *-ila*, etc.; present tenses in *-it*, *-yat*, *-aet*, *-ayut*, and many other overwhelmingly repetitious forms), either by using it as seldom as possible or by enriching it with a *consonne d'appui*. Although in *EO* poor verbal rhymes, as well as poor noun rhymes (in *-an'e* and *-en'e* corresponding roughly to "-ition" and "-ation," and case endings, such as *-oy*) are perhaps more frequent than our poet's miraculous art might warrant, the above-mentioned tendency obtains too, even in such passages in which the deliberate listing of actions or emotions makes it difficult to avoid monotony of rhyme.

In scooping at random a handful of rhymes from *EO* we can sift out such rich ones as:

> *piróv* ("of feasts")
> *zdoróv* ("in good health")
>
> *zevál* ("yawned")
> *zal* ("of halls")
>
> *da-s* ("yessir")
> *glas* ("voice")
>
> *króv'yu* ("blood," instr.)
> *Praskóv'yu* (fem. name, acc.)
>
> *nesnósnïy* ("odious")
> *sósnï* ("pine trees")
>
> *istór'ya* ("story")
> *Krasnogór'ya* (place name, gen.)
>
> *dovólen* ("pleased")
> *kolokólen* ("of steeples")
>
> *ráda* ("glad," fem.)
> *maskaráda* (gen.)

and the best rhyme in the whole poem:

> *síniy* ("blue")
> *Rossíni*

There is also an abundant crop of weak or poor rhymes such as:

> *Richardsóna* (acc.)
> *Grandisóna* (acc.)
>
> *blízhe* ("nearer")
> *nízhe* ("lower")

easy case endings:

> *umóm* ("mind," instr.)
> *litsóm* ("face," instr.)

the easy and inexact:

> *provórno* ("nimbly")
> *pokórna* ("submissive")
>
> *priézd* ("arrival")
> *prisést* ("a sitting down")

and banal rhymes such as:

> *lyubóv'* ("love")
> *króv'* ("blood")
>
> *óchi* ("eyes")
> *nóchi* ("nights")

In English, fancy rhymes or split rhymes are merely the jester bells of facetious verselets, incompatible with serious poetry (despite Browning's talented efforts to glorify them). The Russian Pushkin can quite naturally and artistically rhyme *gdé vï–dévï* ("where are you"–"maidens"), but the Englishman Byron cannot get away with "gay dens"–"maidens."

The beginning of Four : XLIV contains one of the most ingenious rhymes in the whole of *EO*, an unexpected but at the same time completely natural and delightful chiming of a foreign name with a very Russian locution accented on the preposition:

> *Pryamím Onégin Chíl'd Garól'dom*
> *V dalsyá v zadúmchivuyu lén':*
> *So sná sadítsya v vánnu só-l'dom,*
> *I pósle, dóma tsélïy dén'* . . .

which means (in free iambics, unrhymed):

> Onegin like a regular Childe Harold
> lapsed into pensive indolence:
> right after sleep he takes a bath with ice,
> and then remains at home all day . . .

but all Byron could have achieved, had the roles been reversed, might have resulted in the burlesque:

> And similar to the boyar Onegin,
> . . . . . . . .
> With a cold bath my Harold would the day 'gin

or perhaps he might have rhymed "licent" with "ice in't" (for other remarks on this curious subject see my n. to Four : XLIV : 1). Another striking rhyme in the same canto, st. XLIII, coming on the heels of a quip regarding weak rhymes, is *W. Scott–raskhód*, an ear rhyme with the second word sounding *ras-hót*, a comic echo of the English writer's name.

A few words remain to be said concerning the long rhyme. Since so many thousands of Russian words are accented on the antepenult, or incur this accent by inflection, a long rhyme, especially a weak one (e.g., *nézhnïe–myatézhnïe*, "tender–restless," or *piláyushchiy–mechtáyushchiy*, "the flaming–the dreaming"), is easier to find and is used far more extensively in Russian than in English. Nor does it have in Russian any particular association with the extravagant and the trivial. It was neither rich nor popular during the first third of the last century, but then steadily increased in fancifulness and charm with poets experimentally inclined. Probably the most famous short poem in long rhyme (alternating with masculines) is Blok's *The Incognita* (*Neznakomka*), a set of iambic tetrameters in which the rhymal concatenation of extra syllables looks like the reflection of lights in the suburban puddles of the poem's locus. The long rhyme, however, leads to a deadly monotony of rhythm in a protracted piece, whereas its more striking specimens (Fet's *skrómno tï–kómnatï*, "demurely you–room," or Blok's *stólikov–królikov*, "of tables–of rabbits") become so closely associated with the poems in which they were initially used that their occurrence in later verse inevitably sounds like a reminiscence or an imitation. The quest for spectacular rhymes eventually led Russian poets to the incomplete or assonant rhyme, but this matter lies outside the scope of our present inquiry.

The reader should be careful not to confuse the scudded masculine rhyme with the long rhyme. In the following example, all six lines are in iambic tetrameter, with a long rhyme in 1 and 3, a masculine rhyme in 2 and 4, and a feminine rhyme with contraction in 5 and 6.

> The man who wants to write a triolet,
> When choosing rhymes should not forget
> That some prefer a triple violet
> And some a single violet;
> Nor should he spurn the feminine vi'let
> Blooming, contracted, on its islet.

The fact that the rhyme, no matter its length, lies outside the metrical scheme of the line leads to some droll results. If we devise, for example, an iambic couplet in which the rhyme is not merely long, but monstrous and, indeed, a very sea serpent in length, we shall see that despite there being six additional syllables after the ictus, making fourteen syllables in all of the line, the latter still remains a tetrameter (or "octosyllable," as some would call it):

> *Est' rífmï próchnïe, napráshivayushchiesya,*
> *I mnogonózhki ést', podkáshivayushchiesya*

which means, in prose, "There are solid rhymes that suggest themselves readily, and centipedes, whose legs buckle under them." This couplet is identical in metrical length with, say:

> *Est' rífmï tóchnïe, i ést'*
> *Drugíe. Vséh ne perechést'*

which means, "There are exact rhymes, and there are other ones. All cannot be listed."

*Index*

*Devoted to the literary materials chiefly.*

## A

Academy of Sciences, *see* St. Petersburg
*Allegro, L'*, *see* Milton
Anna Ivanovna / Ioannovna, Empress, 38; *see also* Lomonosov
Arnold, Matthew, 64, 67; *Resignation*, 17, 66–7
*Auf den zwischen Ihre Röm. Kaiserl. Majestät und der Pforte An. 1718 geschlossenen Frieden, see* Günther
*Au Roy Henry le Grand, sur la prise de Marseille, see* Malherbe

## B

Baratïnski, Eugeniy Abramovich, 50n
Batyushkov, Konstantin Nikolaevich, 44, 80
Belïy, Andrey, *see* Bugaev
*Belle Dame Sans Merci, La, see* Keats
Berberov, Nina Aleksandrovna, 33n
Blake, William, 78
Blok, Aleksandr Aleksandrovich, 50n, 78, 80, 81; *Incognita, The (Neznakomka)*, 94
Boileau-Despréaux, Nicolas, 41, 45; *Ode sur la prise de Namur*, 42–3 & n
*Break, Break, Break, see* Tennyson
Bridges, Robert: *Milton's Prosody*, 20
*Brief Guide to Rhetoric, A (Kratkoe rukovodstvo k ritorike), see* Lomonosov
*Bronze Horseman, The, see* Pushkin
Browning, Robert, 66, 68, 93;

*One Word More*, 78; *Porphyria's Lover*, 9, 17, 66
Bugaev, Boris Nikolaevich ("Andrey Belïy"), 14 & n, 15, 42, 48n; *Simvolizm (Symbolism)*, 14n
Butler, Samuel: *Hudibras*, 17, 50, 53, 57–8, 63
Byron, George Gordon, Baron, 64, 93; *Isles of Greece, The*, 67; *Mazeppa*, 64

## C

*Canterbury Tales, The, see* Chaucer
*Captain's Daughter, The, see* Pushkin
Castalian Fountain, 40
Chaucer, Geoffrey, 32; *Canterbury Tales, The*, 32; *Hous of Fame, The*, 51–2
*City of the Plague, The, see* Wilson
Civil War (Russian), 89
Clough, Arthur Hugh, 67
Coleridge, Samuel Taylor, 25, 57, 78; *Pains of Sleep, The*, 9, 17, 63–4
*Confessio amantis, see* Gower
*Convent Threshold, The, see* Rossetti
Cotton, Charles, 58, 59; *Entertainment to Phillis, The*, 59; *New Year, The*, 59; *Retreat, The*, 59; *Valedictory*, 59
"Count Null," *see* Pushkin
Cowper, William, 62; *Olney Hymns*, 62; *Written After Leaving Her at New Burns*, 17, 62

## D

*Daisy, The, see* Tennyson
Danzig, ode on, 43n

*Definition of Love, The, see*
    Marvell
*Demon, see* Lermontov
Derzhavin, Gavrila Romano-
    vich, 40, 43, 44, 80
Dolgoruki, Prince Ivan Mihay-
    lovich: *Fireplace in Moscow*
    (*Kamin v Moskve*), 23n
*Dolores, see* Swinburne
*Domik v Kolomne, see* Pushkin
Donne, John, 56; *Extasie, The*,
    16, 17, 49, 56
Dyer, John, 61; *Grongar Hill*,
    61

### E

*Elegy II, see* Trediakovski
Eliot, T. S., 53; *Mr. Eliot's*
    *Sunday Morning Service*, 50n
*Entertainment to Phillis, The*,
    *see* Cotton
*Epitaph, An, see* Prior
*Eugene* / *Evgeniy Onegin* (*EO*),
    *see* Pushkin
*Eve of St. Mark, The, see* Keats
*Evgeniy Onegin, see* Pushkin
*Extasie, The, see* Donne

### F

*Fairy Tales, see* Pushkin
*Feast at the Time of the Plague,*
    *The, see* Pushkin
Fénelon, François de Salignac
    de la Motte-, 42
Fet, A. A., *see* Shenshin
*Fireplace in Moscow, see*
    Dolgoruki

### G

*Garden, The, see* Marvell
*Gde ni gulyayu, ni hozhu, see*
    Sumarokov
*Good-Night to the Season, see*
    Praed

Gower, John: *Confessio aman-*
    *tis*, 31
*Graf Nulin, see* Pushkin
*Grongar Hill, The, see* Dyer
Günther, Johann Christian:
    *Auf den zwischen Ihre Röm.*
    *Kaiserl. Majestät und der*
    *Pforte An. 1718 geschlossenen*
    *Frieden*, 41–2
*Gypsies, The, see* Pushkin

### H

Hodasevich / Khodasevich,
    Vladislav Felitsianovich, 33n,
    50n; *Sobranie stihov* (Collected
    Verses), 33n; "Years have
    from memory eroded" (*Iz*
    *pamyati izgrizli yodi*), 33
Hotin / Khotin, *see* Lomonosov,
    *Hotinian Ode*
*Hotinian Ode, see* Lomonosov
*Hours of Fame, The, see*
    Chaucer
Howard, Henry, Earl of Surrey;
    *Lover Describeth His Restless*
    *State, The*, 8, 54–5
*Hudibras, see* Butler

### I

*Incognita, The, see* Blok
*In Memoriam, see* Tennyson
*Isles of Greece, The, see* Byron
*Iz pamyati izgrizli godi, see*
    Hodasevich

### J

Johnson, Samuel, 61; *On the*
    *Death of Dr. Robert Levet*, 61

### K

*Kamin v Moskve, see* Dolgoruki
*Kapitanskaya dochka, see*
    Pushkin

Keats, John, 57, 65; *Belle Dame Sans Merci, La*, 65; *Eve of St. Mark, The*, 9, 64–5
Khotin, *see* Hotin
*King Lear*, *see* Shakespeare
*Kratkoe rukovodstvo k ritorike*, *see* Lomonosov

# L

*Last Love*, *see* Tyutchev
Lenski (*EO*), 70, 72, 73
Lermontov, Mihail Yurievich, 50n, 78; *Demon*, 50n
*Letter about the Rules of Russian Versification*, *see* Lomonosov
Lomonosov, Mihail Vasilievich, 34, 39–40, 80; *Brief Guide to Rhetoric, A* (*Kratkoe rukovodstvo k ritorike*), 39–40, 44; *Collection of Various Works*, 40; *Letter about the Rules of Russian Versification* (*Pis'mo o pravilah rossiyskogo stihotvorstva*), 39, 44–50; *Ode on the Anniversary of the Ascent to the All-Russian Throne of Her Majesty Empress Eliza-veta Petrovna, All-Russian Autocratrix* (*Ode to Empress Elizabeth*) (*Oda na den' vosshestviya na vserossiyskiy prestol eyo velichestva Imperatritsi Elizaveti Petrovni, samoderzhtsi vserossiyskiya, 1746*), 17; *Ode to the Sovereign of Blessed Memory Anna Ioannovna on the Victory over the Turks and Tatars and on the Taking of Hotin* (*Hotinian Ode*) (*Oda blazhenniya pamyati Gosuda-rine Imperatritse Anne Ioannovne na pobedu nad turkami i tatarami i na vzyatie Hotina 1739 goda*), 33, 39–44
*Lover Describeth His Restless State, The*, *see* Howard

# M

Malherbe, François de, 40, 41; *Au Roy Henry le Grand, sur la prise de Marseille*, 42–3 & n
Marvell, Andrew, 53, 59, 64; *Definition of Love, The*, 49; *Garden, The*, 16; *Nymph Complaining for the Death of Her Fawn*, 17; *To His Coy Mistress*, 9, 58
*Mazeppa*, *see* Byron
*Mednïy vsadnik*, *see* Pushkin
*Metrical Guide to Pushkin's Poems* (*Metricheskiy spra-vochnik k stihotvoreniyam A. S. Pushkina*, N. V. Lopatin, I. K. Romanovich, & Yarho, V. I.), 70
Milton, John, 6, 57, 78; *Allegro, L'*, 56–7; *Penseroso, Il*, 16
*Milton's Prosody*, *see* Bridges
*Molva* (Report, suppl. of *Teleskop*, ed. Nadezhdin), 80
Morris, William, 68; *Old Love*, 67–8
*Mr. Eliot's Sunday Morning Service*, *see* Eliot

# N

N., Princess (in *EO*), 71
Nekrasov, Nikolay Alekseevich, 48n
*New and Brief Method of Russian Versemaking*, *see* Trediakovski
*New Year, The*, *see* Cotton
*Neznakomka*, *see* Blok
North, Christopher, *see* Wilson
Northumbrian Psalter, 39n
*Noviy i kratkiy sposob k slozheniyu rossiyskih stihov*, *see* Trediakovski
"No wonder winter glowers," *see* Tyutchev

*Nymph Complaining for the Death of Her Fawn, The, see* Marvell

# O

*Oda blazhennïya pamyati . . . Hotina (Hotinian Ode), see* Lomonosov
*Oda na den' vosshestvïya . . . , see* Lomonosov
*Oda o sdache goroda Gdanska, see* Trediakovski
*Ode on the Surrender of the Town of Gdansk, see* Trediakovski
*Ode sur la prise de Namur, see* Boileau
*Ode to Empress Elizabeth, see* Lomonosov
*Ode to the Sovereign of Blessed Memory Anna Ioannovna . . . on the Taking of Hotin, see* Lomonosov
*Old Love, see* Morris
Olga (in *EO*), 70, 71
*Olney Hymns, see* Cowper
Onegin, Evgeniy (in *EO*), 70–74, 91, 93
*Onegin's Journey, see* Pushkin
"Onegin's Letter," 71, 76
*On the Death of Dr. Robert Levet, see* Johnson
*One Word More, see* Browning

# P

*Pains of Sleep, The, see* Coleridge
Parnassus, Mt., 40
*Penseroso, Il, see* Milton
*Pir vo vremya chumï, see* Pushkin
*Pis'mo o pravilah rossiyskogo stihotvorstva, see* Lomonosov
Poland, Russian war with, 43n
*Poltava, see* Pushkin

*Porphyria's Lover, see* Browning
*Poslednyaya lyubov', see* Tyutchev
*Povest' o gore i zloschastii, see* Tale of Grief and Ill-Fortune
Praed, W. M.: *Good-Night to the Season,* 10n
Prior, Matthew: *Epitaph, An,* 59–60
Prokopovich, Feofan, 35
Pushkin, Aleksandr Sergeevich, 3, 6, 33, 41, 44, 45, 48, 50n, 58, 63, 69, 70, 77, 80, 91; *Bronze Horseman, The (Mednïy vsadnik),* 70; *Captain's Daughter, The (Kapitanskaya dochka),* 26; *Eugene / Evgeniy Onegin (EO),* 3, 4, 17, 21–7, 30, 49, 52, 54, 55, 68–76, 82, 87, 91–4; *Fairy Tales (Skazki),* 78; *Feast at the Time of the Plague, The (Pir vo vremya chumï),* 26; *Graf Nulin* ("Count Null"), 88; *Gypsies, The (Tsïganï),* 79; *Onegin's Journey,* 25, 72, 76; *Poltava,* 70; *Ruslan and Lyudmila,* 23; *Small House in Kolomna, A (Domik v Kolomne),* 70

# R

*Resignation, The, see* Arnold
*Retreat, The, see* Cotton
*Reverie of Poor Susan, The, see* Wordsworth
Rïleev, Kondratiy Fyodorovich, 26
Ronsard, Pierre de, 40
Rossetti, Christina: *Convent Threshold, The,* 91
*Ruslan and Lyudmila, see* Pushkin
*Russian Versification, see* Unbegaun

## S

St. Petersburg, 70; Academy of Sciences (Nauk), 39

Saintsbury, George, 21, 68

Shakespeare, William, 31, 55; *King Lear*, 18n; Sonnet CXLV, 55

Shenshin, Afanasiy Afanasievich ("Fet"), 48n, 94

*Silentium, see* Tyutchev

*Simvolizm, see* Bugaev

*Skazki, see* Pushkin

*Small House in Kolomna, A, see* Pushkin

Sonnet CXLV, *see* Shakespeare

*Sovremennik* (The Contemporary, first ed. Pushkin), 80

*Stella's Birth-day, see* Swift

Sumarokov, Aleksandr Petrovich, 24, 45–6; "Wherever ramble I or go" (*Gde ni gulyayu, ni hozhu*), 45–6

*Sunday Homilies*, 39n

Surrey, Earl of, *see* Howard, Henry

Swift, Jonathan: *Stella's Birth-day*, 60

Swinburne, Algernon Charles: *Dolores*, 78

*Symbolism, see* Bugaev

## T

*Tale of Grief and Ill-Fortune, The* (*Povest' o gore i zloschastii*) (anon.), 34

*Tale of a Usurer* (anon.), 39n

Tatiana (in *EO*), 70, 71, 73

"Tatiana's Letter," 76

Tennyson, Alfred, Lord, 68; *Break, Break, Break*, 29; *Daisy, The*, 16; *In Memoriam*, 9, 15–16, 17, 65–6

*To His Coy Mistress, see* Marvell

Trediakovski / Tred'yakovski, Vasiliy Kirilovich, 36–9, 44, 45, 78; *Elegy II*, 38; *New and Brief Method of Russian Versemaking* (*Noviy i kratkiy sposob k slozheniyu rossiyskih stihov*), 36; *Ode on the Surrender of the Town of Gdansk* (*Oda o sdache goroda Gdanska*), 43n

*Tsigani, see* Pushkin

Tyutchev, Fyodor Ivanovich, 48n, 50n, 80; *Last Love* (*Poslednyaya lyubov'*), 80; *Silentium*, 80; "No wonder winter glowers" (*Zima nedarom zlitsya*), 77

## U

Unbegaun, Boris, 23n; *Russian Versification*, 23n

## V

*Valedictory, see* Cotton

Voloshin, Maksimilian Aleksandrovich, 89

Vyazemski, Prince Pyotr Andreevich, 26

## W

"Wherever ramble I or go," *see* Sumarokov

*Whirl-blast from Behind the Hill, A, see* Wordsworth

*White Doe of Rylstone, The, see* Wordsworth

Wilson, John ("Christopher North"): *City of the Plague, The*, 26, 27n

Wordsworth, William, 63, 64; *Reverie of Poor Susan, The*, 79; *Whirl-blast from Behind the Hill, A*, 62–3; *White Doe of Rylstone, The*, 63

*Written After Leaving Her at New Burns, see* Cowper

# Y

Yalta, 89
Yazïkov, Nikolay Mihaylovich,
   50n
"Years have from memory
   eroded," *see* Hodasevich

# Z

Zaretski (in *EO*), 72
Zemfira's song, 79
Zhukovski, Vasiliy Andreevich,
   44, 45, 80
*Zima nedarom zlitsya, see*
   Tyutchev

*ABRAM GANNIBAL*

## Abram Gannibal

---

FOREWORD

*Pridyót li chás moéy svobódï?*
Will [it] come the hour of my freedom?

*Porá, porá!— vzïváyu k néy;*
Time, time!—I call to it;

*Brozhú nad mórem,*[1] *zhdú pogódï,*
I roam above the sea, I wait for the [right] weather,

4 *Manyú vetríla korabléy.*
I beckon to the sails of ships.

*Pod rízoy búr', s volnámi spórya,*
Under the cope of storms, with waves disputing,

*Po vól'nomu raspút'yu mórya*
on the free crossway of the sea

*Kogdá zh nachnú ya vól'nïy bég?*
when shall I start [on my] free course?

8 *Porá pokínut' skúchnïy brég*
Time to leave the dreary shore

---

1. The numeral "10" attached to "sea" in the established text
refers the reader to Pushkin's note: "Written in Odessa"; i.e.,
on the northern shore of the Black Sea, in 1823.

> *Mne nepriyáznennoy stihíi,*
> of a to me inimical element,
>
> *I sred' polúdennïh zïbéy,*
> and 'mid the meridian ripples,
>
> *Pod nébom Áfriki moéy,*
> beneath the sky of my Africa,[2]
>
> 12 *Vzdïhát' o súmrachnoy Rossíi,*
> to sigh for somber Russia,
>
> *Gde yá stradál, gde yá lyubíl,*
> where I suffered, where I loved,
>
> *Gde sérdtse yá pohoroníl.*
> where [my] heart I buried.
>
> —*Evgeniy Onegin,* One : L

The following sketch, which deals mainly with the mysterious origin of Pushkin's African ancestor, has no pretensions to settle the many difficulties encountered on the way. It is the outcome of a few odd moments spent in the admirable libraries of Cornell and Harvard universities, and its purpose is merely to draw attention to the riddles that other workers have either ignored or answered wrongly. Although in several instances I have keenly felt the want of original documents, preserved in Russia (where, it seems, they are inaccessible even to native Pushkinians), I am consoled by the fact that any material pertaining to any research is incomparably easier to obtain in the institutions of this country than in those of a wary police state. A list of some of the works consulted in the present case will be found at the end of these notes.

PUSHKIN'S COMMENTS PUBLISHED DURING HIS LIFETIME

Pushkin's n. 11 to *EO*, One : L : 11 ("... my Africa"), reads in the 1833 edn.: "The author, on his mother's

---

2. Here another numeral, "11," refers to a note discussed further.

side, is of African descent," and in the 1837 edn.: "See
the first edition of *Eugene Onegin*," which is a reference
to the 1825 (Feb. 16) separate edition of Chapter One,
in which there is a long note (written probably in mid-
October, 1824,[3] and certainly after Aug. 9, 1824, the
date of his arrival at his estate Mihaylovskoe (near
Opochka, province of Pskov) from Odessa, and presumably before his brother's departure for Petersburg, in
the first week of November, with the apograph of the
canto), based mainly on the MS biography in German
of his maternal great-grandfather. Pushkin's note reads:

The author, on his mother's side, is of African descent.
His great-grandfather, Abram Petrovich Annibal,[4] in his
eighth year was kidnaped on the coast of Africa[5] and
brought to Constantinople. The Russian envoy, having
rescued [*vïruchiv*] him, sent him as a gift to Peter the
Great,[6] who had him baptized[7] in Vilno. *In his wake, his
brother arrived, first in Constantinople, and then in St.
Petersburg, with the offer to ransom him; but Peter I did
not consent to return his godchild.*[8] Up to an advanced age,
Annibal still remembered Africa, the luxurious life of
his father, and nineteen brothers, of whom [sic] he was
the youngest; he remembered how they used to be led
into his father's presence with their hands bound behind
their backs, whilst he alone remained free and went
swimming under the fountains [or "cascades"] of the
paternal home; he also remembered his beloved [or

3. Old Style (Julian calendar) is used throughout for the dating
of events in Russia.
4. This is the French form of the English and German "Hannibal" and of the Russian "Gannibal" or "Ganibal"; we
should constantly bear in mind that our poet's classical education was entirely dependent on French versions of, and French
commentaries on, the ancients. See further my discussion of
Abram's assumed surname.
5. Or, lexically, "was stolen from the shores of Africa."
6. Peter I, emperor of Russia, reigned 1682–1725.
7. *Krestil ego*, which also implies "godfathered him."
8. Here, and elsewhere in Pushkin's notes, I have italicized
passages that are not supported by, or are in blatant contradic-
tion to, possible or actual facts, as discussed further.

"favorite"] sister, *Lagan'*,[9] swimming in the distance after the ship in which he was receding.

At *eighteen*, Annibal was sent by the tsar to France, where he began his military service in the army of the regent; he returned to Russia with a slashed head[10] and the rank of French lieutenant [Fr. *capitaine*]. Thenceforth he remained *continually* near the person of the tsar. *In the reign of Anna*,[11] Annibal, a personal enemy of Bühren,[12] was dispatched, under a specious pretext, to Siberia. *Getting bored with an unpeopled place and a harsh climate, he returned to St. Petersburg of his own accord and appeared before his friend Münnich.*[13] *Münnich was amazed and advised him to go into hiding without delay. Annibal retired to his country estates and dwelled there all through the reign of Anna, while nominally serving in Siberia.* When Elizabeth ascended the throne, she lavished her favors upon him. A. P. Annibal lived to see the reign of Catherine II, when, relieved of important duties of office, he ended his days with the rank of general in chief, dying in his *ninety-second year* [in 1781]. [An authorial footnote to this reads: "We hope to publish in due time his complete biography."]

His son, Lieutenant General I. A. Annibal, undoubt-

---

9. An inept, albeit traditional, Russian transliteration; the name is spelled "Lahann" in the German biography.

10. The fact of his having been wounded seems to be supported by the headaches he suffered in later years. The regent was Philippe d'Orléans, who ruled from 1715 to 1723, during the minority of Louis XV.

11. The succession of royal personages in Russia during Gannibal's lifetime was: Catherine I, Peter's widow (r. 1725–27); his grandson, Peter II (r. 1727–30); Anna, daughter of Ivan, Peter I's, brother (r. 1730–40); Anna, daughter of Charles Leopold, Duke of Mecklenburg-Schwerin, and Peter I's grandniece, regent (1740–41) during the minority of her son, who never reigned; Elizabeth, Peter's daughter (r. 1741–61); another grandson of Peter's, Peter III (1761–62); and Catherine II, called the Great (r. 1762–96), self-made widow of Peter III.

12. Anna's powerful favorite; in Russian, Biron; Ernst Johann Bühren, Duke of Courland (1690–1772).

13. In Russian, Minih. Burkhard Christoph, Count Münnich (1683–1767), field marshal.

edly belongs to the number of the most distinguished men of Catherine's age. He died in *1800*.

In Russia, where the memory of eminent men is soon obliterated owing to the absence of historical memoirs, the bizarre life of Annibal is known only through family tradition.

PUSHKIN'S ANCESTORS

On the Russian nobility side, Pushkin's family name can be traced back to one Konstantin Pushkin, born in the early fifteenth century, younger son of a Grigoriy Pushka. From Konstantin, there is a direct line of descent to Pyotr Pushkin (d. 1692), the ancestor of both parents of our poet (the paternal great-grandfather of his father and the maternal great-great-grandfather of his mother).

Pyotr Pushkin's son, Aleksandr (d. 1727), was the father of Lev (d. 1790), who was the father of Sergey (1770–1848), who married Nadezhda Gannibal (1775–1836) in 1796 and fathered our poet, Aleksandr Pushkin (1799–1837).

Pyotr Pushkin's younger son, Fyodor (d. 1728), was the father of Aleksey (d. 1777), who was the father of Maria (d. 1818). Maria Pushkin married Osip Gannibal (1744–1806), third son of Avraam Petrov, alias Gannibal, a Russianized African (1693?–1781). Osip's and Maria's daughter, Nadezhda, married Sergey Pushkin (her mother's second cousin) and was our poet's mother.

Abram (Avram, Avraam, Ibragim) Petrovich, or Petrov (baptismal patronymic), Annibal, or Gannibal, or Ganibal (assumed surname), hereafter referred to as "Abram Gannibal," had eleven children by his second wife, Christina Regine von (?) Schöberg, or Scheberch (b. 1706, d. two months before her husband): among them, Ivan Gannibal (1731?–1801), a distinguished general; Pyotr Gannibal (1742–1825?), artillery officer and country squire; Osip Gannibal (1744–1806), also a military man of sorts, our poet's maternal grandfather (in 1773 he married Maria Pushkin, second cousin of Sergey Pushkin); and two obscurer Gannibals, Isaak (1747–1804) and Yakov (b. 1749).

The following notes, in so far as my own research goes, mainly concern the origins and the first third of Abram Gannibal's life.

### THE DOCUMENTS

The basic documents regarding Abram Gannibal's origins are:

The petition: a clerical copy of a petition addressed in February, 1742 (i.e., in the reign of Elizabeth, Peter's daughter), by Major General Abram Gannibal, *ober-komendant* of Revel, or Reval (now Tallin), NW Russia, to the Senate, applying for a nobleman's diploma and heraldic arms.

The German biography: ff. 40–45 of a manuscript some 4000 words long (classified in the Lenin State Library, Moscow, as Cahier 2387A, which is a batch of sheets sewn together, to form a book, by the police immediately after Pushkin's death), comprising an anonymous biography of Abram Gannibal, written in a small Gothic hand, and pompously worded in idiomatic but none-too-literate German. All we know about this German biography (the MS of which I have not seen) is that it was written after Abram Gannibal's death (1781); that it contains certain details, such as a few names and dates, that only Gannibal would have remembered; and that it also includes a number of passages, contradicted either by historical documents (such as Gannibal's own petition) or by plain logic, that were obviously inserted by the biographer with a view to pad the story, to span its gaps, and to give a eulogistic (but actually absurd) interpretation of this or that event in the hero's life. I think, therefore, that whoever spun this grotesque fabric had before his or her eyes some autobiographic notes left by Gannibal himself. The German seems to me to be that of a Rigan or Revalan. It may be the work of some Livonian or Scandinavian relative of Mme Gannibal (née Schöberg). The bad grammar seems to preclude its being a professional genealogist's job.

Pushkin's n. 11 to *EO* (mainly based on the biography, but with some new details supplied by family tradition or romantic imagination) has already been quoted.

We have in addition four items, curious and important in themselves, but not casting any new light on the subject: (1) an anonymous, very clumsy and incomplete, Russian version of the German biography, on ff. 28–29 and 56–58 of the same Cahier 2387A, in Pushkin's hand, but obviously dictated to him, judging by the uncouth style, probably in October, 1824, and certainly not later than the end of the year, by someone who had more German than he, with some desultory marginalia by Pushkin; (2) a very brief *curriculum vitae*, written or dictated to somebody by Pyotr Gannibal in his old age,[14] when he lived near the Pushkins' Mihaylovskoe, at his small countryseat, Petrovskoe; (3) a few words concerning Abram in a genealogical note, written by Pushkin in the early 1830's, known as *Rodoslovnaya Pushkinïh i Ganibalov*, in which a short passage concerning Gannibal begins: "My maternal great-grandfather was a Negro . . ." (same Cahier 2387A, ff. 25, 60, 26, 59, 62); and (4) the factual as faintly seen through the fictional in Pushkin's unfinished historical romance (1827), six chapters and the beginning of a seventh, published

---

14. In a letter dated Aug. 11, 1825, Pushkin wrote to his country neighbor, Praskovia Osipov: "I plan to look up my old Negro great-uncle, who, I suspect, will die one of these days: I am anxious to obtain from him certain memoirs regarding my great-grandfather." Was this all he was able to get?

posthumously (1837) as *Arap Petra Velikogo* (The Blackamoor of Peter the Great), in which Abram appears as Ibragim (Ibrahim, Turkish form of Abraham).

### DATES OF ABRAM GANNIBAL'S BIRTH AND DEATH

The three biographers nearest to Gannibal in time, Helbig (see "Works Consulted"), the unknown author of the German biography (c. 1785), and Bantïsh-Kamenski (1836), are not in agreement. Helbig says that Abram died in 1781, and reckons his age at eighty-seven. The German biography says he died May 14, 1781, in his ninety-third year, which would have made him about seventeen years old when he first arrived in Moscow, whereas the same document says that he was "unter zehn Jahren" at the time, and in his twenty-eighth year in 1723–24. Bantïsh gives the date of Abram's death as 1782 and his age as ninety-one (a figure he obtained presumably from Pushkin's published note of 1825). This gives us a range of possible birth dates between 1689 and 1697; I am inclined to take 1693 as the nearest to historical truth.

On the grounds of Pushkin's marginalia in Cahier 2387A (as given in the descriptions of that MS), we can establish the fact that, except for the German biography, our poet had no chronological information regarding his great-grandfather's origin and youth. When beginning (July 31, 1827) his historical romance *"Arap Petra Velikogo,"* Pushkin attempted to calculate Gannibal's birth and death dates from the scanty and conflicting data of the German biography (he appears not to have known, or to have ignored, Helbig at the time). In the margin of the first page of the Russian version of the German biography (f. 28 in the batch of sheets in the order in which they were posthumously sewed), our poet computed that if Abram was twenty-eight in 1725 (which would make him only eighty-four at the time of his death), he must have been born in 1697, and at the age of nine (in accordance with the statement in the German biography, a statement that might have set the numerative ball rolling in the first place) was brought to Russia in "1708" (either a mere slip for the correct 1706 or wishful miscalculation). Like many great men, Pushkin was a sedulous and wretched mathematician.

In another abstruse task—namely, at the top of the fourth page of the abridged Russian version of the German biography dictated to him (2387A, f. 56)—our poet apparently attempted to find the date of Gannibal's birth if, say, he were not twenty-eight, but twenty-six, in 1725. He discovered this to be 1699 and, adding nine, obtained the desired "1708," the year in which he thought that Gannibal had been baptized immediately upon his arrival in Russia.

A cryptic note in the right-hand corner of the second page (2387A, f. 57) reads: "brought [to Constantinople] [1]696," which is evidently the result of reckoning based on the fact that the German biography says that Gannibal was seven when removed from Abyssinia and ninety-two at the time of his death. We do not know how Pushkin coped with the awkward mathematical consequence that makes the little Moor spend ten years in the sultan's seraglio and appear as a gangling youth of seventeen before the tsar in Moscow. The only other jotting of interest is the name "Shepelyov," written in the left-hand margin of the same page. It would seem that Pushkin thought Dmitri Shepelyov (d. 1759)[15] to have been the Russian envoy at the time in Turkey. The envoy was, of course, Pyotr Tolstoy.

---

15. As *gofmarshal* (earl marshal, master of ceremonies), Shepelyov accompanied Peter I on his journey to western Europe in 1716–17; he was made a general by the tsar's daughter, Elizabeth, in 1743.

### GANNIBAL'S ORIGIN

The German biography begins: "Awraam Petrowitsch Hannibal war . . . von Geburt ein Afrikanischer Mohr [a blackamoor, an African black] aus Abyssinien. . . ."

This fact therefore was known to Pushkin (who took down the Russian translation), but nowhere in his own notes does he ever refer to a specific region when speaking of his ancestor.

The *EO*, Chapter One, note (see earlier, "Pushkin's Comments . . .") begins: "The author, on his mother's side, is of African descent."

Aleksey Vulf, in an entry in his journal, mentions retrospectively that Pushkin showed him, on Sept. 15, 1827, at Mihaylovskoe, "the two first chapters he had just written of a romance in prose [now known as *Arap Petra Velikogo*], in which the main character represents his great-grandfather Gannibal, the son of an Abyssinian emir, captured by the Turks and sent from Constantinople by the Russian ambassador as a gift to Peter I, who had him educated and grew very fond of him."

In the Russian version of the German biography our poet's unknown dictamentor translates "Afrikanischer Mohr" "African Negro." And the German biography itself, in a further passage, refers to Gannibal as a *Neger*.

Abyssinians (or Ethiopians, in the strict sense) have a skin color varying from dusky to black. Their type represents a Hamito-Semitic component of the Caucasian race; and a Negroid strain may so strongly predominate in some tribes that the term "Negro" is in such cases applicable in a general sense; but apart from these considerations (to which I shall return at the end of these notes), the European layman of the time—and, in fact, Abram Gannibal himself—would classify colloquially as a "Negro" or "blackamoor" (in Russian, *negr* or *arap*—note the ultima) any more or less dark-skinned African who was not an Egyptian and not an Arab (in Russian, *arab*).

In his brief *curriculum vitae*, in badly misspelled Russian, written or more probably dictated in his dotage, Pyotr Gannibal makes the following statement (probably in the autumn of 1825, when our poet presumably consulted him):

My father . . . was a Negro; his father was of noble origin; that is, a ruling seigneur. My father was taken as an *amanat* [a Caucasian term meaning "hostage"] to the court in Constantinople, whence he was stolen and dispatched to Tsar Peter I.

This is repeated in Pushkin's note *Rodoslovnaya . . . Ganibalov.*

The German biography continues thus:

[He was] the son of a local ruler, powerful and rich, who proudly traced his descent in direct line from the house of the famed Hannibal, the terror of Rome. [Abram's] father was a vassal of the Turkish emperor or the Ottoman Empire who by the end of the preceding century, because of oppression and molestation [*Druck und Belästigung*], had revolted, with other Abyssinian princes, his countrymen and allies, against his overlord, the sultan; whereupon various petty but bloody wars followed, in which, however, might eventually triumphed and this Hannibal [Abram], still a boy, the youngest son of the ruling prince, with other highborn youths, was sent in his eighth year to Constantinople as a hostage. Although, given his youth, this fate should not have befallen him so early, still, owing to the fact that his father, according to the Moslem custom, had very many wives (even up to about thirty, with a correspondingly large progeny), the numerous old princesses and their children joined forces in the common intention of protecting themselves and their offspring; and since [Abram] was the youngest son of one of the youngest wives, who did not have at court as many supporters [as the elder princesses had], these contrived through trickery and intrigue, almost by force, to put him on a Turkish vessel

[*Fahrzeug*] and turned him over to the fate that had been assigned him.

I shall presently show that in the 1690's, the period referred to here, no Abyssinian was a vassal of the Ottoman Porte, and no Abyssinian prince could have been a Moslem or could have been forced to send any tribute to Constantinople. The "terror of Rome" will also be discussed. But before I attempt to clear up all this muddle, let us glance at the geographical situation.

### GANNIBAL'S BIRTHPLACE

Abram Gannibal's petition (1742) contains the following brief but important information:

I, your humble subject, am a native of Africa [*rodom ya . . . iz Afriki*], of the high nobility there [*tamoshnego znatnogo dvoryanstva*]. I was born in the demesne [*vo vladenii*] of my father, in the town of Lagona [or Lagono or Lagon: *v gorode Lagone*—this is the locative case, which in Russian does not disclose the ultima of the nominative]. Moreover, my father had under his rule [*imel pod soboyu*] two other towns . . .[16]

It will be noted that (in so far as we have to rely on this text as it appears in the various biographical works listed at the end of this appendix—e.g., Anuchin) no particular region in Africa is indicated in the petition. On the strength of the German biography, I assume that this town is in Abyssinia. The locative case, as already stated, does not provide one with any clue to the orthography of the nominative; moreover, the ridiculous Russian custom of transliterating both *h* and *g* by means of a Russian gamma does not tell us whether this African name in a Roman transcription[17] should be "Lagon,"

---

16. For the next sentence of the petition see the section "Gannibal and Raguzinski."

17. I.e., the characters universally accepted in geographic

"Lahon," "Lagona," "Lahona," "Lagono," or "La-
hono." I suspect that "Lahona" is the correct transcription of the unknown original but shall further refer to
the place as "L." The similarity between the name of the
sister mentioned in the German biography and the name
of the native town mentioned only in the petition is very
disturbing. I have not found—within the limited scope
of my reading—any instance of an Abyssinian child
receiving the name of its birthplace.

In the course of a work that in its historical, ethnical,
and geo-nomenclatorial portions is below criticism,
Dmitri Anuchin (1899), an anthropologizing journalist,
states that after talking to a "French traveler, Saint-
Yves" (Georges Saint-Yves?), and to "Professor Pau-
lichke" (presumably, Philippe Paulitschke), he has
come to the conclusion that "L" is a town and a district
located "on the right bank of the river Mareb in the
province of Hamasen." The "Loggo" supplied by
Paulitschke (teste Anuchin), and also by an Italian map
of 1899 (which I have not seen), and the "Logo" of Salt
(to be discussed presently), somehow, in the course of
Anuchin's comments and deductions, evolve first a
caudal *t* and then a caudal *n*, which none of *my* "L's" do;
for at this point I abandoned Anuchin and launched
upon some research of my own.

Charles Poncet (traveling in 1698–1700) divides the
empire of Ethiopia into several kingdoms (provinces),
such as the Tigré. He divides the Tigré (ruled by Viceroy
"Gaurekos") into twenty-four principalities (districts),

---

nomenclature. This has nothing to do with individual mistakes
or transliterative predilections (Latin, Spanish, Italian, German, English, French, etc.) within the range of this alphabet,
or the tendency on the part of experts in this or that language
transliterated to break into a rash of diacritical signs. This
writer fervently hopes that the Cyrillic alphabet, together
with the even more absurd characters of Asiatic languages,
will be completely scrapped some near day.

of which he names only a few, such as the "Saravi" (Serawe), a plateau 6000 feet high.

Henry Salt, a century later, divides the Tigré proper ("commonly called the Kingdom of the Baharnegash") into less than half of Poncet's number of districts, among which he names the Hamazen in the north, the Serawe south of it, and, still farther south, the tiny district of Logo. At some later date, when the Hamazen (or Hamasen) and the Serawe became provinces, the latter, in its spread or shift southward to the Mareb River, engulfed the Logo district and other small districts.

The Mareb is easily located, and its name hardly varies in travelers' accounts, of which there are so few prior to the nineteenth century. An examination of the reproductions of the old maps in the splendid work of Albert Kammerer (1952) shows that this is the Mareb of Jacopo d'Angiolo (alias Agnolo della Scarperia), Rome MS, c. 1450; of Melchisedec Thevenot (after Balthazar Tellez), 1663; of Job Ludolf, 1683; of Bourguignon d'Anville, 1727; of Bruce, 1790 (drawn 1772); it is the Marib of Fra Mauro, 1460; the Marabo of Jacopo Gastaldi, 1561; the Marabus of Livio Sanuto, 1578; the Marab of Father Manoel de Almeida, 1645 (sketched c. 1630). It is also the Moraba of Poncet's account (1704).

Anuchin's informer, or more probably Anuchin himself, has confused two separate places: Logo and Logote. Saint-Yves, traveling, I suppose, sometime in the latter part of the nineteenth century, had seen from a mesa (Tokule Mt.) the town of "Logot" (teste Anuchin, Russian transliteration) in the valley of the Mareb. In Salt's time (1810), Logo and Logote (or Legote) were separate townlets in two adjacent districts, the northern Logo and the southern Legote, the latter bounded south by the Munnai stretch of Mareb River. According to the only other author who mentions Logote (T. Lefebvre,

1846, III, 21, 28; whom, no doubt, Anuchin's French informer had read), the district of Logote (Salt's Legote) is separated from the districts of "Tserana" and "To-koulé" by the Belessa River (which is the Mai Belessan of Salt (1816 edn., p. 195), a tributary of the Mareb. Lefebvre describes the Belessa as following the example of the Mareb by disappearing under the sands during the dry season, when, however, a little digging provides one with plenty of water. "Cette vallée de Logote étant très malsaine et remplie d'animaux carnassiers [lions, panthers], tous les villages sont situés sur la chaine," and the villagers, having to come from those arid heights for water into the valley, are "très avares de leurs provisions."

The Mareb, which in its central course may be roughly said to separate northern Abyssinia from the rest of the country, is at various seasons and at various points of its meandering progress a raging torrent, an underground stream, or a dribble losing itself among the sands. Its various stretches bear, or have borne, local names. Its headwaters arise in the northeast, within fifty miles of Annesley Bay on the Red Sea; it is a tiny rivulet with a narrow bed below Debarwa; then it swells, sweeps south, turns west, and, collecting numerous other streams from the northern mountains, flows west toward the Sudan frontier, to disappear in the soil near Kassala, though in very wet weather an ultimate trickle reaches Atbara. Among these little northern tributaries we find the Seremai, the Belessa, and the Obel. The last appears on Bent's map (1893) and on the U. S. Army map (1943); the Seremai River, which is apparently just east of the Obel, is mentioned by Salt (1814), who, on his way inland from the Red Sea and the town of Dixan, which he left Mar. 5, 1810 (p. 242), arrived the following day at the picturesque village of Abha (p. 245):

March 7th.—We struck our tents at five in the morning, and after proceeding about a mile southward, brought the hill of Cashaat to bear due east of us, at which point . . . we turned off a little to the west, and travelled about eight miles . . . until we reached an agreeable station, by the side of a river called Seremai. This river shapes its course through the bottom of a small secluded valley, surrounded on every side by steep and rugged hills, in a nook of which, about a mile to the eastward, lay a large town called Logo, whence the surrounding district takes its name.

Logo at that time (1810) was commanded by a rebellious chieftain "who in the campaign of the preceding year had been reduced to obedience by the Ras," and who made an attempt to stop and rob Salt's caravan. For all we know, he may have been Pushkin's fourth cousin.

From Logo the Salt party traveled SSW (p. 248) "Our road now [Mar. 7, 1810] lay . . . through a wild and uncultivated country; we crossed the stream called Mai Belessan . . . and, after mounting a steep ascent, reached the village of Legóte. . . . The distance we had travelled from our last station [on the Seremai River, one mile west from the village of Logo] may be computed at about eight miles." Salt then crossed the Mareb and proceeded southward toward the "completely scarped" mountain (Debra Damo), "which in the earliest periods of the Abyssinian history, served as a place of confinement for the younger branches of the [royal] family" (p. 248), at which point Salt recalls Dr. Johnson's "beautiful and instructive romance." This is a reference to Samuel Johnson's insipid tale, *The Prince of Abissinia* or (in later editions) *The History of Rasselas, Prince of Abissinia*,[18] which appeared anonymously in two volumes

---

18. *Rasselas* was represented in Pushkin's library (Ballantyne's Novelist Library, vol. V, London, 1823, which also contains Sterne's *Sentimental Journey* and Goldsmith's *The Vicar of Wakefield*), but Pushkin had not enough English to

in the spring of 1759—at a time readers managed to find poetry and talent in the journalism of Voltaire's flat *Contes*. Earlier (1735) Johnson had translated for a few shillings Joachim Le Grand's *Voyage historique d'Abissinie, du R.P. Jérôme Lobo*, Paris, 1728 (and this is the explanation of the spelling "Abissinia" in *Rasselas*, which puzzled James Macaulay, author of the preface to the 1884 facsimile edition of that work). Jeronimo Lobo, whose own text has never been printed, was a Portuguese Jesuit; he visited Abyssinia during the years 1624–32, in the reign of Susneyos (Malak Sagad III, later known as Seltan Sagad I), who publicly made his submission to Rome; the hero of Johnson's tale was that emperor's brother, Ras (Prince) Ce'ela Krestos (spelled also Cella Christos), the Rasselas of Le Grand (p. 502), governor of Gojam, and one of the stanchest supporters of the Jesuits (Beckingham and Huntingford, 1954, pp. xxv, 59). It is most pleasing to reflect that Salt may have seen on the very same day the birthplace of Pushkin's ancestor and the scene of Johnson's story.

The only maps on which I have been able to locate Logo are: the one in Salt's work and a smaller one (obviously copied from Salt, without acknowledgment) illustrating the 1830–32 journal kept by Samuel Gobat (a Swiss clergyman born in 1799). On Salt's map, this townlet or village of Logo is situated at 39°2′5″ E and 14°7′5″ N. It lies about forty-five miles NNW of Aksum and about fifty miles S of Debarwa. I doubt if it exists today;

---

read it. If he knew Johnson's tale at all, as he probably did, it was in a French translation, of which there were several (Belot, 1760; Fouchecour, 1798; Louis, 1818; Notré, 1823). A Russian translation was published in Moscow, 1795, but a Russian gentleman would ignore the wretched Russian adaptations of the time and prefer the more fluid, though hardly more exact, French versions. Thus the poet and rebel Küchelbecker read *Rasselas* in French in prison, at Sveaborg, Feb. 2, 1832.

perhaps it has wandered to some other site, as Abyssinian villages have been known to do; but its ghost should be sought N of the Munnai stretch of the Mareb River and E of its little northern tributary, the Obel (*obel* means "tamarisk" in Tigré), in the former province of Seraoe (Serae, Serawe). On Baratieri's map (1896) there is a "Mai Laham" at 38°7′ E, 14°7′5″ N, and on the U. S. Army map (1943), there is an "Adi Mai Laam" on the "Asmara" at 38°9′ E, 14°8′ N. *Adi* means "village," *mai* is "water" or "ford," *laham* may be "cattle" or (according to Salt, 1811, III, 12) a "mango-like tree" (which is, I presume, *Eugenia owariensis* Beauv.). On none of the numerous maps made prior to the eighteenth century have I found any locus suggestive of "Logo," or "Lagon," or "Lagona," except obvious Italian or Spanish descriptive terms for "lake," "canal," "hot spring," or "pool" (*lagone*).

The trouble is that at exactly the necessary period, between the last visits of Jesuit priests in the 1630's and James Bruce's travels in the 1770's, no vocal European except Poncet (1698–1700) journeyed to northern Abyssinia—and neither Lobo (in Le Grand), nor Almeida, nor Poncet, nor Bruce mentions "L."

I have discovered, however, another candidate for Gannibal's birthplace. Salt, in his earlier journal (1811, III, 61), mentions the village of "Lahaina,"[19] which he saw on Sept. 9, 1805, on his way northward from "Anta-low" (Antalo), the capital of Tigré-Endorta, to "Muc-cullah" (Macalle), in the same province. This Lahaina is, or was, about six miles from Antalo, in a direction nearly NNE, and thus about a hundred miles SSE of Logo. I cannot locate it on any map, but judging by

---

19. Or is this a misspelling for "Lahama" or "Lehama," a small district in Endorta mentioned by Lefebvre (III, 43)? There is, of course, another "Lahaina" in the world—namely, the former residence of the kings in the Hawaiian Islands.

Salt's account (he had just passed by "a picturesque village called Haraqué," which I identify with Gargara of the U. S. Army map, 1943), I should place Lahaina midway between 39° and 40° E and midway between 13° and 14° N. Beyond "Haraqué," after proceeding from one hill to another, Salt saw "on a rising ground to our right [to the east] a village of considerable extent called Lahaina, from which place the road, turning a little more to the west, led through a more cultivated country, thickly set with acacia and brushwood . . ." There is no reason why this Lahaina, rather than Logo or Logote, should not have been the Lagona or Lahona of Gannibal's petition, and there may have existed other similarly sounding place names (on a "Laham" basis, for instance). I would consider therefore the determination of "L" as not settled at the time of writing (1956); but I am inclined to assume that it was situated in the general region of northern Abyssinia, where we have been following, through the bibliographic dust, the mules and camels of several adventurous caravans.

GANNIBAL'S SISTER

After the passage concerning the scheming senior wives, who managed to have the youngest one's son turned over to the Turks, the German biography continues thus:

His only full sister, Lahann, who was some years older than he, had yet sufficient courage to oppose this act of violence. She tried everything, but had to yield to number; she accompanied him to the very deck of the small ship, still nursing the hope that she might obtain by entreaties the freedom of this much beloved brother or purchase it with her jewels; but when she found that her tender efforts [*zärtliches Bemühen*] remained fruitless to the last, she cast herself in despair into the sea and was drowned. To the very end of his days, the venerable old man [Abram] would shed tears of the tenderest friendship and love as he recollected her; for although he was still very young at the time of that tragic event, yet whenever he thought of her this vague memory would become new and complete for him; and this offering [Abram's tears] was the better deserved by her sisterly tenderness since she had struggled so hard to free him, and since these two were the only siblings from the same mother.

Pushkin, in his note to the 1825 edn. of Chapter One of *EO*, obviously improves upon the German biography when he says: "[Abram] also remembered his beloved [or "favorite"] sister, *Lagan'* [Russ.], swimming in the distance after the ship in which he was receding."

As I have already mentioned in a footnote to his *Lagan'*, Pushkin carelessly follows here the Russian tradition of rendering the Latin *H* by the Russian gamma (so that, for instance, Henry becomes *Genri* and Heine masquerades as *Geyne*). Moreover, he attempts to feminize the ending of the name, which terminates in a consonant (an impossible ending for a feminine name in Russian), by closing it with a "soft sign" (an apostrophe in transliteration).

The receding ship, in whose wake swam—somewhat ahead of the romantic era—a passionate sister, might be easily condemned to dwindle to a reed raft on a seasonable river; indeed, the entire event might be dismissed by the cynic as one of those fairy-tale recollections that old age confuses with true happenings; but there is one reason it should command attention: the name "Lahann" is, I find, a plausible Abyssinian name.[20]

Generally speaking, names in *L*, and particularly in

---

20. In Turkish, a language that Gannibal must have been able to understand at one time, *lahana* means "cabbage" and *lahin* "note," "tone," "melody." In Arabic, *lahan* means "melody," "modulation," "mispronunciation," and *layan* means "softness," "gentleness," *Zärtlichkeit*. In several Oriental languages, the stem *lah-* is associated with "loose woman" (cf. the Russian *lahanka*, a slattern, Pskovan dial., and *lahudra*, an inferior whore).

*La*, occur comparatively seldom in Abyssinian chronicles. According to Amharic dictionaries, there is a man's name "Layahan"; and in the reign of King Bahafa (1719–28) there was a general named Lahen, who died about 1728 when governor of Hamasen (R. Basset, 1881, XVIII, 363).

We do not know how old was Ras Fares, governor of Tigré, in the 1690's, nor do we know the number of his wives or concubines. But we do know that Fares must have been an elderly man at the time, and we also know from the chronicles (Basset, XVIII, 310) that a young wife of his, who died at the latest in 1697, bore the name of Lahia Dengel or Lahya Dengel (meaning in Tigré "beauty of the Virgin"), which has a striking resemblance to that of the girl who may have been her daughter.

### GANNIBAL'S PARENTAGE

To understand the various improbabilities and absurdities in the German biography, the history of Abyssinia should be briefly recalled.

The Gospel was introduced there about A.D. 327 by Frumentius (c. 290–c. 350), a native of Phoenicia, who was consecrated bishop of Aksum by Athanasius of Alexandria. An awareness of that primitive empire, so near to Arabia, so far from Rome, was slow in reaching western Europe. The first reliable information was the fortunate outcome of ill-fated ventures on the part of heroic Jesuit missionaries who affronted the nameless dangers of a fabulous land for the holy joys of distributing images of their fair idols and of secretly rebaptizing native children under the pious disguise of medical care. Some of these brave men were successful as martyrs, others as mapmakers. In the sixteenth century, Portuguese troops helped the Abyssinians to break a relatively brief spell of Moslem domination that began about 1528 and lasted till the middle of the century. At one time, c. 1620, under King Susneyos, Abyssinia was actually converted by Portuguese Jesuits into a grotesque form of Catholicism, which petered out about 1630, in the beginning of the reign of Fasilidas, who restored the old religion and had the churches occupied again by the Monophysite clergy. In modern times, Russians have been pleasantly surprised at finding a kind of natural Greek-Orthodox tang to certain old eremitic practices still persisting in Ethiopia; and Protestant missionaries have been suspected by the natives of paganism because of their indifference to pictures of female saints and winged boys.

In the period that alone interests us—the last years of the seventeenth century and the first ones of the eighteenth—most Abyssinians were Christians; i.e., members of the Abyssinian Church, a dreary, Coptic-flavored brew of the more absurd ideas of old Christian and Jewish priests, all this spiced with barbarous local abominations. Despite the memory of cruel invasions, the state tolerated, for commercial reasons, Moslems and, for sporting ones, heathen Negro tribes, such as the Shangalla group, to which belonged the black savages inhabiting at the time a region not far from, or including, Logo, at a point "where the river Mareb, leaving Dobarwa, flows through thick bushes" (Bruce, 1790, II, 549). In the late seventeenth century, and afterward, these heathens were enthusiastically hunted by Abyssinian kings in periodical safaris, and there is nothing impossible in a hypothesis that Pushkin's ancestor was captured in the process and sold to the Turks.

By 1700, little trace remained of the Moslem invasion that had been led by Ahmed ibn Ibrahim el Ghazi, sur-named Gran (Lefty), possibly a Somali, more than a century and a half before. Indeed, by the time of John I (c. 1667–81), the Moslems, although holding the east-coast islands, had no political power inland and were compelled to live in separate quarters in Abyssinian towns. It is conceivable that Gannibal's father was a pagan warrior or a well-to-do Moslem trader, and it is likewise conceivable that he was a local chief of princely blood, ruling over a district or a province, but it is impossible for one to imagine (as does Anuchin, blindly followed by Vegner and other ovine compilers) that about 1700, some 150 miles north of Gondar, the proud capital of Abyssinia, and less than 50 miles north from her sacred city Aksum, an Abyssinian nobleman governing three towns would be a subject of the Turkish sultan and thus a vassal of the Ottoman Empire!

We shall now suppose that (1) Gannibal's father was indeed a regional governor in northern Abyssinia and that (2) Gannibal's recollection of "taxes" and "tributes" corresponded in a twisted and nebulous way to certain historical realities.

Gannibal was born in a town beginning with *L*, in the Tigré proper or the Tigré-Endorta, about 1693, in the reign of Jesus the Great (Jyasu I; throne name, Adyam Sagad I), who succeeded his father John in 1680 (according to Basset), 1681 (according to J. Perruchon), or 1682 (according to Beckingham and Huntingford) and was assassinated in result of the machinations of Queen Melakotawit (Fr. transliteration), who wanted her son, Tekla-Haymonot, to reign. Poncet, when spending the summer of 1700 in Debarwa, then the capital of Tigré, feasted there with two regional governors: one of them was apparently the governor of the whole Tigré province (*bahrnegas* or *bahr-negus*, a title that originally meant "lord of the sea," but that by the beginning of the preceding century had lost much of its importance); the other chief was either a temporary coruler or a district governor. Poncet gives the name of the first as "Gaurekos." This, I suspect, should read

"Gyorgis" (or "Guirguis"[21]), which is the Arabic Jirjis and the European George.

The chronicle published by Basset mentions only one governor of Tigré about 1700, namely, Ras Fares (*ras* or *raz* meaning "head" in the Geez language). He became governor in the eleventh year of the reign of Jesus I and was still governor in the twenty-second year of that reign. In the first years of the eighteenth century he seems to have been assigned to other, presumably military, duties, although exercising his governorship off and on; and perhaps the other fellow, George, ruled in the intervals—and was being broken in at the time Poncet found the *bahrnegas* twinned.[22] Ras Fares survived the two-year-long reign of Tekla-Haymonot I and was exiled to the isle of Mesrah by the next emperor, Theophilus (Tewoflos), who reigned for three years (c. 1708–11). At this point I lose track of Fares, who presumably died in exile.

Jesus I (1682–1706, according to Beckingham and Huntingford and to Budge) was a not-untalented despot, and a mighty hunter, inordinately fond of chasing the buffalo and the Galla. He also kept a sharp eye on his provincial and district administrators. In the seventeenth year of his reign—that is, in the late 1690's (when Gannibal was five or six years of age)—the exactions of the officials and their robbery of the nation in collecting taxes became so outrageous that the emperor summoned all the notables from Endorta and other districts and

---

21. The Portuguese Jesuit Almeida, who journeyed inland from the Red Sea in 1621, mentions Keba Christos, governor of Tigré, "encamped in a beautiful meadow near Debaroa [Debarwa]," and Asma Guirguis, his brother.

22. Poncet later met "Guarekos'" brother, an eremite whom he saw in September on his way to Massawa and the Red Sea, in the Monastery of Bizen (Debra Bizan, near Asmara), where the sixty-six-year-old holy man was making himself dreadfully ill by trying to subsist on a diet of raw rack-tree leaves.

demanded an explanation of them. The principal article
of merchandise was rock salt. The officials, in the name
of customs dues, used to confiscate most of the salt that
the merchants brought on their asses into the town. The
emperor decided that the tax on salt should be uniform
throughout the country. The tax on five mules laden
with salt was to be one slab (see Basset, XVIII, 303–20,
and Budge, I, 417).

The scandal coincided with Poncet's arrival in Abyssinia, and it is possible to believe that Ras Fares and
various district governors in the province of Tigré (including Endorta) were involved. In these cases the
emperor would no doubt feel even freer than usual to
exact tribute from the governors—and probably would
think nothing of ordering them to send their children as
samples of Abyssinian nobility to the court of a Frankish
king.

### GANNIBAL'S ENSLAVEMENT

In the Abyssinia of those days everybody seems to have
been selling everybody else into slavery. There is a
charming story about an Abyssinian priest who is sent
young divinity students by a friend, another priest, sells
these youths one by one to a Moslem trader, then sells
him his friend the priest, and then gets sold himself.
In his *Travels* (1790), Bruce mentions Dixan (at 14°59′55″
and 39°38′30″, according to Salt), the first frontier town
he reached in Abyssinia from the coastal island of
Masuah (Massawa), on the Red Sea. "Dixan is built on
the top of a hill, perfectly in form of a sugar loaf" (III,
84), and consists of Moslems and Christians; "the only
trade of either of these sects is a very extraordinary one,
that of selling of children. The Christians bring such
as they have stolen in Abyssinia to Dixan as to a sure
deposit; and the Moors receive them there, and carry

them to a certain market at Masuah, whence they are sent over to Arabia and India" (III, 88).

About 1700, according to Poncet, the price for a robust male slave was only ten *écus* (fifty shillings). In 1880, according to Enid Starkie, the average price of a small boy was twenty strips of copper cut from a kettle. Some eight years later, in the days of "trader Rainbow" (as the English called the French ex-poet Rimbaud), Christian Abyssinian boys cost eighty Levant dollars (about 150 shillings) per head. One suspects that most of the little Africans shipped to Arabia and Turkey were used there as catamites before reaching the age of toil.

I do not know how probable it may have been for the child of a seigneur, a province governor, or district governor to be directly or indirectly sold into slavery; but there is definite information (for instance, in Poncet) that in 1700 Emperor Jesus could and did command the noblemen—i.e., various relatives of his, as all nobles were—to dispatch their children to a distant European court, with the result that these unfortunate Abyssinian youngsters were captured en route by the Turks.

Poncet, a French pharmacist in Cairo, who was invited to Abyssinia to treat Jesus I for conjunctivitis, left Cairo June 10, 1698, and, via the Nile and Dongola, reached Gondar July 21, 1699. The emperor proclaimed a young Armenian merchant (named "Murat" or, more exactly, Murad ben Magdelun, said to be the nephew of one of the emperor's ministers) ambassador to France: he was to accompany Poncet to Paris with gifts for King Louis XIV such as elephants, horses, and *jeunes enfans éthiopiens*, scions of noble families.

On his return voyage to Cairo (now via the Red Sea), Poncet left Gondar May 2, 1700, for Massawa, planning to stop on the way in the capital of Tigré, Debarwa, which he reached in mid-July, and to wait there for

Murad, who was still collecting the animals and the children. But there were further delays; several horses and the only elephant, a young tuskless beast, died while crossing the Serawe Mts., and on Sept. 8, 1700, after waiting for Murad for almost two months, Poncet left Debarwa for the coast. Nine days later he reached the island of Massawa, embarked for Jidda on Sept. 28, and arrived there on Dec. 5. Murad being still delayed, the next meeting place was fixed at the head of the Red Sea in Suez, for which Poncet set out Jan. 12, 1701. At the end of April he reached the Mt. Sinai Monastery, where a month later Murad finally caught up with him, bringing a sad report: in Jidda, "le Roy de la Mecque" (the Grand Sherif Saad?) took away from him the highborn Ethiopian children that Murad had collected for the king of France—and it is not inconceivable that some of these the governor of Mecca (or that of Jidda) forwarded to the sultan of the Ottoman Empire, Mustafa II, as his own little tribute. All Murad now had were two young attendants obtained on the way at Suakin, "the bigger one an Ethiopian, the smaller a [Negro?) slave" (Le Grand, p. 431). Poncet's and Murad's caravan reached Cairo in the first week of June, and Poncet presented himself there before the French consul, Maillet.

In Cairo Poncet, now impatient to leave for France, got into trouble with Maillet, who questioned Murad's ambassadorial status, and with the Turks, who questioned the religion of the two slave boys (Murad's acquisition?) whom Poncet was taking with him. Says Le Grand (pp. 417–18): "L'Aga et les gens de la Douane [vinrent] l'avertir [June 26, 1701] que ses deux domestiques Abissins étant Mahométans devoient etre rachetés . . . [Poncet] répondit que si ces enfans étaient Mahométans" he would make a gift of them to the Turkish governor of Egypt. But the local Jesuit superior, "touché de zèle pour le salut de ces deux enfans," intervened, and Poncet was not bothered any more. Whether he got the two youngsters out of Cairo, we do not know. It is also not clear if we should count as one of these boys or count separately as a third item, or consider as representing both, a "jeune esclave éthiopien" (Le Grand, p. 432) whom Murad had brought to the French consul at Cairo, to be shipped to France together with the remains —ears and trunk—of the young elephant. This *petit esclave*, when already placed on the Nile barge that was to take him to the ship, began to cry that he was a Moslem, that he was being kidnaped, that he did not want to go to Christendom, which provoked a tumult, in consequence of which the Turkish officials removed the boy from the barge and placed him in the keep of one Mustafa Kiaya Kazdugli, after which Poncet sailed for France. Incidentally, the episode is curiously distorted in its retelling by Bruce (II, 488–89), who says that Poncet, when embarking at Bulaq, on the Nile, for his voyage to France, "watched helplessly as a bought slave, a poor Abyssinian lad, whom he was bringing for Louis the Fourteenth . . . was being taken out of ship by the Janizaries . . . and made a Mahometan before his eyes"—which implies, if I correctly understand what Bruce means, that the boy was an uncircumcised heathen Negro, and not a Christian Ethiopian, who would have been circumcised anyway (on the eighth day after his birth).

GANNIBAL IN TURKEY

After describing Lahann's death at the time of her brother's departure from Abyssinia or some neighboring seaport, the German biography continues:

Not long after [*nicht lange nach*] this separation forever, Hannibal arrived in Constantinople and with the other young hostages was confined in the seraglio, to be raised there among the noble pages of the sultan, and there he spent one year and some months [*ein Jahr und etliche Monate*].

Let us pause here for a moment in order to check the chronological situation. We shall see presently that the Russian envoy could have obtained the young *arap* only between the autumn of 1702 and the summer of 1705 and that the most probable year is 1703. Working backward, we arrive at the following conclusion.

The journey from his home in inner Abyssinia— which, according to the German biography, Gannibal was forced to leave at seven years of age ("in seinem achten Jahre . . . nach Constantinopel gesandt")—to Turkey must have taken considerably longer than the meaningless gap-filler "nicht lange nach" implies— even if we choose for him the shortest itinerary of the time, from the Tigré Province to northwestern Turkey. There was an initial trek to a Red Sea port, then the tricky passage up the Red Sea to Suez, then another land journey to a Mediterranean port, and finally the long, awesome, and nauseous voyage to Stambul. Taking into account the difficulties of navigation and many delays, we must reckon the whole journey to have lasted at least one year—probably longer, especially if we take into consideration that Gannibal might have been conveyed to Turkey not by sea but by the caravan road via Arabia and Syria. In other words, he must have left home in 1700 if, by 1703, he had been living in Constantinople since the end of 1701.

We now have to choose between two possibilities: (1) that the boy landed in the Constantinople slave market in the ordinary course of the trade or (2) that, as the German biography avers, he was smuggled out of the sultan's seraglio and delivered to the Russian envoy, with the help of a grand vizier.

If we consider the first proposition, all we can say is either that the Russian envoy's agent may have induced his employer to show more gratitude by persuading him that the young slave had really been a highborn prisoner in the palace or, more likely, that the Russian envoy, having purchased the boy by ordinary means, cooked up the exotic version to impress the tsar. Since, however, we are inclined to accept the story of Gannibal's noble origin, for want of a better hypothesis, we may as well see what historical background there is to support the contention of the German biography, which, after the sentence referring to the length of time spent by Gannibal in Constantinople, launches upon the account of his deliverance with the following idiotic argument:

At that time the Emperor Peter I [was] introducing the arts and the sciences in his realm and endeavoring to spread them among [his] noblemen. He did succeed to some extent in this undertaking; yet considering the great multitude of nobles in that most extensive of the world's empires, the number of people who showed inclination toward learning proved much too insignificant, a state of affairs that caused the late emperor most grievous and vexing pain. He cast around for means to extract from among the nation . . . examples and models. Finally, he conceived the idea of writing to his ambassador in Constantinople, requesting him to obtain for him and send him some young black boys of good abilities. His minister followed his orders with the utmost fidelity: he got acquainted with the supervisor of the seraglio where the sultan's pages were being reared and educated, and then, through the intermediation of the grand vizier obtained, in a secret and dangerous manner, three lads. . . .

One of these was Gannibal.

Prior to the era of more or less normal diplomatic relations between Russia and Turkey, a councilor of Peter I, Emelian Ukraintsev (1660?–1708), had been sent as envoy extraordinary to Constantinople in 1699, after the cessation of a long and confused war.[23] He

---

23. The Karlowitz Treaty between Turkey on one side and Austria, Poland, and the state of Venice on the other was

concluded a peace treaty (July 3, 1700), supposed to be good for thirty years, and returned to Russia.[24] In 1700–01 Russia was briefly represented at the Porte by the grand envoy, Prince Dmitri Golitsïn (1665–1737), who was in Constantinople only to ratify the treaty.

The first regular Russian ambassador to reside in Turkey (where he stayed for twelve years) was Count Pyotr Tolstoy (1645–1729), who was appointed Apr. 2, 1702, and arrived in August. The sultan in power, Mustafa II, had one more year to reign before being dethroned (Aug. 22, 1703), in consequence of a thirty-six-day-long military rebellion, by his brother Ahmed III (who was to last till 1730). Mustafa granted Tolstoy his first audience in November, 1702. During the period interesting us (1702–05), seven grand viziers succeeded one another.

Of these, Hussein Kuprulu,[25] an intelligent and amiable pasha, retired Sept. 5, 1702. During his rule, the mortality among Turkish poets was, for some reason, very great: as many as twelve died in 1699. The next grand vizier (*krayniy vizir'*, in the Russian of the time) was Daltaban the Serbian, whom European observers

signed the same year. Incidentally, Emelian Ignatievich (patronymic) Ukraintsev is split into three persons in my edition of Hammer-Purgstall (XIII, 37n): the councilors Amilianusch, Ignatodesich, and Oukraintzov!

24. Subsequently this tough politician was appointed to settle the Russian-Turkish frontier on the river Bug, after which he headed the Department of Provisions, was accused of profiteering, and survived a thrashing with *dub'yo* (a collective noun meaning oak cudgels or knotted clubs), to become envoy to Hungary.

25. The transliteration of Turkish names is the whim of this or that European historian, and the right form is hard to choose without special study. Kuprulu, for instance, appears as Koeprulu in Hammer, Kuprulis in Bonnac, and Kiuprili, Koprulu, or Kuprullu in English works on the subject. As in the case of Abyssinian history, there is also a bothersome discrepancy in matters of dates (I have, on the whole, followed Hammer, with some misgivings).

call an illiterate brute, and who among other wise and
important decrees forbade Christians and Jews to wear
kalpaks of red cloth. His bellicose spirit made him un-
popular, and four months later he was quietly strangled
by the palace executioner. He was succeeded on Jan. 25,
1703, by Rami Pasha, said to be an honest and enlightened personage who wrote verse in a polished style. He
fell with his master, Sultan Mustafa. The next grand
vizier (Aug. 23–Nov. 16, 1703), the first to serve Sultan
Ahmed, was a pasha of Russian extraction, Chancellor
Ahmed, a very corrupt, rotund little man, dubbed
Beehive because of his squat shape and his ability to
store up the sweets of life. Less than four months later
he was exiled to Lepanto, after having been made to
disgorge the treasures he had accumulated. His successor, Hasan, a son-in-law of the sultan, reigned for less
than a year (till Sept. 28, 1704). He was a very honest
and comparatively humane pasha of Greek origin and
cannot be suspected of selling the sultan's pages to a
foreigner. His successor was the bad-tempered and
violent Kalailikoz, who detested Frenchmen and Russians and who, in his turn, was succeeded on Dec. 26,
1704, by Baltaji Mohammed (a former governor of Jidda), a wily pasha who lasted till May 3, 1706. During his
rule, not later than the summer of 1705, Abram Gannibal was shipped to Azov, so we do not have to bother
about the next grand vizier (the tyrannic Ali, 1706–10);
but if any of these worthies was involved in Gannibal's
surreptitious removal from the seraglio to the Russian
embassy or to a moored Russian vessel, I would suggest
it was Beehive or Mohammed.

Pyotr Tolstoy is described by historians as a crafty,
unscrupulous, and sinister character. In 1717, he was
sent by the tsar to retrieve Prince Alexis, the heir to the
throne, who had taken advantage of his ferocious sire's
journey abroad to escape from Russia to Austria and

Italy, and whom the tsar's agents tracked down and brought back, in a series of quiet moves marked by the kind of hypnotic tenacity, persuasion, and deceit that we associate today with the forced repatriation of fugitives by Soviet thugs. The man who could lure Alexis from the security of Naples to his terrible fatherland, to be tortured to death there under Peter's supervision, might easily have devised a means to obtain a poor little blackamoor for his master's amusement.

My opinion that the tsar's envoy to the Ottoman Porte obtained Gannibal, by the tsar's order and for the tsar's service, not earlier than 1703 and not later than 1704 is corroborated by Gannibal himself in the following two documents:

(1) In a letter from Paris to Councilor Makarov, dated Mar. 5, 1721 (probably, N.S.), Gannibal mentions that he has served the tsar for seventeen years.

(2) In an address to Empress Catherine I, in 1726 (when presenting her a textbook on military engineering that he had compiled on the basis of his La Fère or Metz notes; see below, "Gannibal in Western Europe"), he mentions that he has lived for twenty-two years *pri dome* (at the domicile, in the entourage, in the household) of the late tsar (who died in 1725).

GANNIBAL AND RAGUZINSKI

"In the meantime," the German biography continues, using its favorite formula:

the father of the late general [of Abram Gannibal], who had been ripe in years and almost senile at the time of [Abram's] departure, died, and the succession of his rule [*Regierung*] fell to the lot of one of Abram's stepbrothers. . . . The Russian envoy, who was glad to observe the will of his emperor, sent to Moscow [the three lads]: Ibrahim Hannibal; another black boy—a compatriot of his of noble birth—who, however, died of smallpox on the way;

and a Ragusan of nearly the same age, i.e., under ten. Although deploring the loss of one of the boys, the emperor was delighted that the two others arrived safely, and took over personally the care of bringing them up; the more eagerly because, as already said, he wished to make examples of them . . . and put [Russians] to shame by convincing them that out of every people, and even from among wild men—such as Negroes, whom our civilized nations assign exclusively to the class of slaves— there can be formed men who by dint of application can obtain knowledge and learning [and thus] become helpful and useful to their monarch. . . . A no mean connoisseur of mankind, the emperor investigated in advance the inclinations of his newly arrived objects [sic]. He destined Hannibal, who was a quick, keen, and fiery young fellow, for a military career; and he destined the Ragusan (later known in Russia as Count Raguzinski), who was of a quieter and more meditative nature, for the civil service.

We can ignore the passage concerning the succession of rule, which is only there to dismiss a possible accusation of secondary abduction, this time on the part of the beloved monarch, and turn to Abram Gannibal's petition (1742). This petition, after mentioning the three towns Abram's father governed (see earlier, "Gannibal's Birthplace"), proceeds thus: "In 1706, at an early age [*v malïh letah*], I set out for Russia from Constantinople, in the retinue [*pri*] of Count Savva Vladislavich, by my own will, and was brought to Moscow. . . ."

The date 1706 refers to his arrival in Moscow. As we shall presently see, he left Constantinople in the summer of 1705. The Ragusan Vladislavich is the same person that the German biography describes as Gannibal's coeval and fellow page, a preposterous allegation that can be explained only as an attempt to puff up the prestige of the biographee by giving him reputable companions in misfortune and fortune. This Ragusan was thirty-seven years old in 1705, when, according to the relevant passage in the German biography, Gannibal was about ten

years of age—or about twelve, according to a more
plausible computation. Curiously enough, Pushkin pre-
serves the fictional synchronization of the two men's
respective ages in his mediocre romance known as *Arap
Petra Velikogo*: when "Ibragim" at the age of almost
thirty (he is "twenty-seven" at the beginning of the
novel, when, c. 1720, he falls in love in Paris with a
French lady) returns to Petersburg in 1723, he sees in
the emperor's palace "young Raguzinski, his former
chum [*bïvshego svoego tovarishcha*]"—who, historically,
was fifty-five years of age at the time.

Who, then, was this Ragusan of the changeable years?

As early as 1699–1700 Ukraintsev had employed in
Constantinople the services of secret agents of Illyrian
extraction. One of these was a Servian trader named
Savva (Christian name) Lukich (patronymic) Vladislavich (surname), known later as Count Vladislavich-
Raguzinski (1668–1738). He was born in Popovo,
Herzegovina, was brought up in his father's merchant
business in Ragusa, and when about twenty-five (thus
in the 1690's) was transferred to Constantinople. Rightly
or wrongly, his father, Luka Vladislavich, considered
himself descending from a Bosnian princely family of
that name. Upon his removal from Bosnia to Ragusa,
he assumed the composite surname Vladislavich-
Raguzinski. His son's title of count, or at least its formal
fixation, seems to have been a favor granted by Tsar
Peter in recognition of Savva's services.

Under Mustafa II and Ahmed III, Turkey exacted a
tribute from Ragusa (e.g., the sum of 4,000 ducats in
1703) as well as from Arab tribes;[26] but (according to

---

26. The Arabs, on the other hand, kept pilfering the yearly
caravan (a stately affair led by a bejeweled camel) that was
sent yearly from Constantinople to Mecca with money for the
poor. Some of this pilfering seems to have been organized from
Constantinople by the grand viziers themselves.

B. H. Sumner, p. 8n) the law for collecting Christian tribute boys, although nominally in existence until 1750, had not been enforced since the middle of the preceding century. There is no reason not to believe that Savva Vladislavich had been dispatched to Constantinople in the natural course of personal adventure and paternal trade; but the fact of there having been Ragusan tribute boys in the past may have somehow influenced the account of Gannibal's boyhood.

On Sept. 25, 1702, a month after his arrival in Turkey, Pyotr Tolstoy wrote to Count Fyodor Golovin, Minister of Foreign Affairs, thus:

A Ragusan dwelling in Constantinople, Sava Vladislavov [sic], who as you know is a good man, has now, by my advice, set out with wares for Azov and from there will proceed to Moscow. [He] is here an infinitely useful person to His Muscovite Majesty.

Sometime in the autumn of that year Vladislavich arrived in Azov with an ostensible cargo of olive oil, cotton, and calico, and eventually (by the first week of April, 1703) reached Moscow, where in result of the secret reports he brought he was made much of by Peter I.

Bringing sables and ermines, Russian fox (white-collar and red) and wolf (Muscovite and Azovan), he returned to Constantinople in 1704 or early 1705, and then in the summer of 1705 set out again for Azov and Moscow, carrying more calico and more secret dispatches from Pyotr Tolstoy as well as a live present for the tsar.

It is evident that Gannibal was obtained sometime between the dates of Vladislavich's two departures from Constantinople. To judge by a letter from the tsar to the Constantinople ambassador's brother, Ivan Tolstoy, commander of Azov, Vladislavich was in Moscow with the reports, and presumably with the little blackamoor, not later than Jan. 12, 1706 (the exact date of his arrival might be easily settled by consulting unpublished papers in the local archives). Vladislavich traveled in 1716–22 on diplomatic missions to Venice and Ragusa and in 1725–28 was envoy to China.

GANNIBAL'S FIRST YEARS IN RUSSIA (1706–16)

At the time of Gannibal's arrival in Russia, Peter was in the midst of the Swedish campaign, with the battle-field—a fluctuating and somewhat phantomic affair—in Poland. He had stayed in Vilno from July 8 to Aug. 1, 1705, and arrived in Moscow (from Grodno) on Dec. 19, 1705, remaining there till Jan. 13, 1706, when he went back, via Smolensk, to the martial sport in Poland. In Moscow he amused himself with establishing an anatomical and biological museum, with a botanical garden in front of it. The young blackamoor was no doubt welcomed as an additional curio. Peter visited Kiev in July–August, 1706, and, traveling north again, was just in time to enjoy watching, on Sept. 11, 1706, the first inundation in "Piterburh" (or "Paradis," as he fondly called the town he had just founded). Especially entertaining was the sight of men and women huddling on the roofs of submerged shacks.

Peter was again in Vilno (on his way back from Warsaw to Petersburg) by Sept. 24, 1707, and stayed there till Oct. 10. It is within these time limits that the, at least, fourteen-year-old Abyssinian was baptized and given the name Pyotr. More or less synchronously (Sept. 27, 1707), his royal sponsor jotted down a little memorandum dealing with the naming of the progeny of Lenita or Lenta (from the Latin *lenis*, "gentle," or *lentus*, "tenacious," "slow"), an English mastiff: two years before (June 30, 1705), in the monastery of Polotsk, the tsar had had this hound maul Theophanus, an outspoken Uniate monk of the St. Basil Order, whom he had then hacked in two with his sword. The pseudo-classical names for her seven pups, which the tsar translated no doubt from some current nomenclator, read—as translated back from Peter's uncouth Russian —Pirrhous (reddish), Eous (dawn), Aethon (bright), Phlegethon (blazing), Pallas, Nymph, and Venus. The eventual surname Annibal given to the blackamoor may also have been thought up by the enlightened monarch, although there are other possibilities (see further, "Gannibal and Annibal"). The fate of the young mastiffs can be traced to another note, a fortnight later (Oct. 10, 1707), in which the tsar commands Lenita's pups to be taught by some foreign-born fancier on his staff to perform various tricks, such as doffing a cap, shouldering a toy musket, and marching under arms into water.

At the time, according to western European observers, reiteration of baptism, and baptism anew, of youths and adults, was performed at Peter's court by pouring cold water three times over the whole body from head to foot. If Gannibal had been born an Abyssinian princeling, he would have been baptized at birth, since Abyssinia had been Christianized six centuries before Russia; but it is quite probable that upon capture the Turks had him Moslemized (*pobasurmanili*, in the Russian of the time), whatever that process implies. The question, however, is completely futile because, first, any African was to Russians a heathen and, second, the ceremony performed on the young blackamoor, at the Pyatnitski church, in late September or early October, 1707 (not "1705," as the memorial plaque there oddly says), with Peter I as godfather and Christiana Eberhardina, wife of King Augustus II of Poland, as godmother (fide the German biography), was conducted in the rowdy and slapstick atmosphere of Peter's court and smacks of mock mar-riages between freaks or the elevation of jesters to the rank of governors of Barataria. Indeed, there seems to have been an attempt by some zealous courtiers, a few months before, to marry the blackamoor: in a letter from Poland, dated May 13, 1707, the tsar writes to Councilor Avtonom Ivanov that he does not wish to have the *arap* conjugated—with, presumably, the daughter of some grandee's Negro servant, or a dwarf, or a Russian female house fool (*domashnyaya dura*, *shutiha*). This was a critical moment for the gene that participated in the making of Pushkin, and the tsar should be thanked for directing the course of chance.

With the light of history now beginning to glimmer upon our subject, we can drop the tedious task of following the burlesque and bombastic German biography, which rambles on for as many pages as I have already quoted or paraphrased. We shall still have to refer to it, however, now and then in connection with certain bothersome trivia. Let us turn to some of the anecdotes about young Gannibal.

The best-known story is one given in preposterous detail by the German biography, and repeated with personal variations by Golikov and Pushkin. The gist of it is that young Abram, upon becoming the tsar's valet or assistant valet, slept in an adjacent room and proved his intelligence by transcribing the drafts of decrees that his master would scribble at night on slates. Among a series of Pushkin's notes entitled "Table Talk" (Eng.), 1836–37, the posthumously published eighth item (1873, in *Vestnik Evropï*), described by Pushkin as "A story [that] is not particularly clean but depicts Peter's ways," reads:

One day a little blackamoor accompanying Peter I on his promenade [canceled beginning: "The blackamoor Gannibal accompanied Peter I on one of his journeys. One day the child"] stopped for a certain need and all at once cried out in terror: "Sir, sir! The gut's a-coming out of me!"

Peter went up to him and, having perceived what the matter was, said: "Bosh, this is no gut, it is a worm," and pulled it out with his own fingers.

In a document dated Dec. 20, 1709 (quoted by M. Vegner, p. 23), a passage reads: "By [the tsar's] order, in view of the Christmas holidays, coats have been made for Joachim the dwarf and Abram the blackamoor, with camisoles and breeches. Moreover, eight arshins [six yards] of scarlet cloth . . . and brass buttons have been purchased for both." E. Shmurlo (1892) vaguely refers to some documents in which "Abram is mentioned three times, in the same breath, with the tsar's jester Lacosta." This is Yan Dekosta or, correctly, Jan d'Acosta, Peter's favorite court jester, a Christianized Jew born in Holland.[27] According to another anecdote, one day in the summer of about 1715, on board ship, just before a royal cruise from St. Petersburg to Revel, the tsar's physician, Lestocq,[28] and a gentleman of the chamber,

---

27. He was a man of parts and a member of a well-known marrano family (da Costa, or Mendez da Costa) that had fled from Portugal in the seventeenth century and settled in Italy, Holland, England, and other countries. Jan d'Acosta, who was a lawyer in Hamburg, sought a more colorful life and finding a patron in the Russian consul followed him to Muscovy. The tsar was delighted with his wit, made him a count, and gave him a barren island off the Finnish coast.

28. The high spirits of this adventurous French nobleman, Count Jean Armand de Lestocq (1692–1767), also known as "Hermann Lestock" and "Ivan Lestok" (he emigrated to Russia in 1713), appealed to the tsar, who nonetheless would give him a sound thrashing now and then. That despot's guffaws and snarls easily intergraded. Dr. Lestocq seems to have been a confirmed jester-baiter, whereas the tsar, on the other hand, had a special tenderness for his fools. In 1719, Lestocq got into trouble with d'Acosta, whose daughter he had seduced. Peter banished his gay bloodletter to Kazan, in eastern Russia, where Lestocq remained till the reign of Elizabeth. The source of the nautical story is a collection of *Anecdotes* pertaining to Russian customs, etc., published (London, 1792) anonymously by a friend of Lestocq, the

Jonson,[29] two merry fellows, having found the tsar's Russian jester Tyurikov fast asleep on the deck, played a period prank upon him: they took some tar and glued his long beard to his bare chest. Upon awakening, the poor jester howled, at which the tsar, interrupted in his studies of navigation and keelhauling, came pounding along, bumped into the innocent Gannibal, and, in a rage, flogged him unmercifully with a length of rope. At dinner the two pranksters could not help chuckling at the sight of the Moor's glum face. When the good tsar, a humorist in his own right, learned the cause of their mirth, he burst out laughing too and told Abram that to mend matters he would ignore his next misdemeanor.

This is about all I was able to gather in the way of published material pertaining to Gannibal's first ten years in Russia. We can dismiss as family fantasy a passage in the German biography that asserts that "the ruling half brother" of Gannibal instructed a young brother to travel to Constantinople to ransom Abram; that, not finding him there, this brother traveled on to Petersburg, bringing as gifts "precious weapons and Arabic writs," which established Abram's princely origin; that the latter refused to go back to heathendom; and that the brother set out on his return journey "with tears on both sides." There is hardly any need to remark that no Abyssinian seigneur could have traveled to Muscovy via Turkey without being enslaved there, nor is there any historical information of any free Abyssinian undertaking such a journey in the first part of the eighteenth century.

It is likely that the tsar took his *arap* along on some of his travels or campaigns, but hardly on all his marches,

---

German and French writer Johann Benedikt (Jean Benoît) Scherer (1741–1824), who came to Russia about 1760 and joined the French embassy in St. Petersburg.
29. The son of a Livonian architect.

as family tradition has it. We get a ghostly glimpse of a stylized young blackamoor in more or less Turkish garb lurking in the emblematic background—holding a battle horse or a bunch of grapes—in several portraits of Peter I. He is present in an engraving executed by Adriaan Schoonebeeck (d. 1705) from a lost picture painted about 1704; there he stands at the back, and to the anatomical right, of the tsar, who, for the nonce, sports a French king's dress. I am not sure there is not some error in the dating of the thing itself or of its engraver's death. But if we accept the date, and the possibility of the pictured blackamoor being Gannibal, we have to suppose that either he was brought by Raguzinski on the latter's first trip to Moscow (1703) or that he was portrayed—prospectively, as it were—on the strength of information received in Moscow from Constantinople: a blackamoor in attendance was a symbol of supreme luxury and grandeur, and the tsar must have awaited his 1706 New Year gift from his envoy with as much eagerness as he did shipments of lilies and lilacs.

### GANNIBAL IN WESTERN EUROPE (1716–23)

In January, 1716, Peter I set out on a European tour. After spending a month or so in Copenhagen, he pursued his journey to Holland and France. He landed in Dunkerque on Apr. 30, 1717, N.S., and arrived May 7 in Paris, where he forthwith asked for beer and bawds. Philippe, Duke of Orléans, was regent of France (1715–23) during the minority of Louis XV. The Muscovite tsar's six-week stay produced little more than a crop of dirty stories—though why the grandees of the Régence, a filthy pack in a disgusting and talentless age, should have been so puzzled by Peter's habits is not quite clear.

In the same spring of 1717, four young men arrived in France from Russia to study fortification and military mining. They may have come with the tsar, but more probably they voyaged separately from him and did not sojourn in Denmark. The four were: Abram Arap, Stepan Korovin, Gavrila Rezanov, and Aleksey Yurov, our hero's chum.

The German biography, with its usual overstatement, bad grammar, and inexactitude, says that Peter I sent Gannibal straight to the Regent, asking the latter "to assume supervision," and that Gannibal at first studied "under the great Belior [sic] at a military school for young noblemen." The reference is, I suggest, to Bernard Forest de Belidor (1693–1761), a brilliant young French engineer who taught at the Ecole d'Artillerie of La Fère (in the Aisne, NW of Laon) and wrote a *Sommaire d'un cours d'architecture militaire, civile et hydraulique* (1720) and other distinguished works. As to the Regent's "personal supervision," I cannot find any indication among French sources that he (or any member of his entourage) was aware of Abram's existence.

According to the German biography, Gannibal then joined an artillery regiment in France and as a *capitaine* of a company participated in a war against Spain. This war was declared Jan. 9, 1719, and peace was signed Feb. 17, 1720. During an undermining operation— somewhere in Catalonia, I suppose—he was severely wounded in the head and taken prisoner (it is odd that he never mentions this event in his letters from France). Upon his return to France, Abram apparently went on with his studies at another school, the Ecole d'Artillerie of Metz, an institution founded by the illustrious mili- tary engineer Sébastien Le Prestre, Marquis de Vauban (1633–1707). According to E. A. Bégin (1829, p. 592), the subjects taught there at the time were mathematics, physics, and chemistry, on Monday, Wednesday, and Friday; "l'école pratique se faisait les autres jours, excepté le dimanche, dans l'île Champière, où existait un parc. . . . Ce n'était, à bien dire, qu'une école régimentaire dont les cours cessaient dès que Metz était privé du corps d'artillerie qui y tenait habituellement garnison."

By January, 1722, the Russian ambassador, Prince V. L. Dolgorukov, had announced to the four young men that they would have to return to Russia, but a year of procrastination followed. It would seem that part of that year Abram and his companions spent in Paris—in the hectic Paris that had been left a financial shambles by John Law. Early spring was marked by fabulous balls and illuminations in honor of the arrival of a tentative bride for the king, the blonde little infanta, aged four and a half, whom, however, the twelve-year-old Louis did not like. The Regent was energetically pursuing his life of debauchery. Courtesans wore stockings of flesh-colored silk. Thieves and highwaymen were subjected to the iron boot, the toasting of toes against an ordinary or extraordinary fire, and foot baths of boiling oil. The financial term "liquidated" (*liquidé*) was used in regard to executed criminals. The poet Arouet (better known as Voltaire) was thrashed by the footmen of an officer whom he had called a police spy. Prodigious sums were won and lost at faro. The Marquis de Saillant successfully wagered he would ride ninety miles on horseback in six hours.

In the midst of these dazzling frolics, little is known of Abram's existence, except that he was continuously and abjectly hard up. I can find nothing in the French memoirs of the Régence that would corroborate statements made by Pushkin in his novel that all the ladies desired to entertain *le nègre du Czar*, that he hobnobbed with Voltaire, and that the playwright Michel Guyot de Merville introduced him to a woman of fashion, "Countess Lénore de D.," who bore him a black baby. The letters Abram wrote in Russian from France to various officials (clamoring for money, pleading not to be sent home by sea, saying he would rather walk than sail, begging in vain to be left in France for further studies, and so forth) seem to me to have been worded not by him but by his companion in hyperbolic distress, Aleksey Yurov. After six or seven years abroad, Abram appears to have forgotten Russian so thoroughly that upon his return the autocrat bundled him off to grammar school at the Aleksandronevskiy Monastery, where he was enrolled on Mar. 14, 1723, O.S. He seems to have been returned to the imperial household on Nov. 27, 1724 (see P. Pekarski, 1862, I, 112). Commentators have wondered if perhaps the event might refer to some other "Abram the blackamoor" (though no other is known), since it seemed to them to clash with the fact that on Feb. 4, 1724, by a ukase in the tsar's own hand Abram ("in dem 28-sten Jahre seines Alters," says the German biography) was made a lieutenant (*poruchik*) in the bombardier company of the Preobrazhenskiy regiment. However, the whole age was a freakish one.

Gannibal brought from France a small library (sixty-nine titles) consisting mainly of historical works, military manuals, travels, and a sprinkling of fashionable exotica; all these volumes he sold (in 1726) for two hundred rubles to the Imperial Library but bought them (or a similar set) back in 1742. Although the list is quite conventional, with works by Bossuet, Malebranche, Fontenelle, Corneille, and Racine representing its literary section, there is a distinct stress on various voyages, with Chardin taking the reader to Persia to discover that a milk diet cures ulcers; Lahontan visiting, in a kind of proto-Chateaubriandesque America (1688), the Gnacsitares and the Mozemleks, whom none saw after him; and Cyrano de Bergerac journeying to the moon, where people have names only expressible by little melodies of a few musical notes.

### GANNIBAL AND ANNIBAL

Officially, the name of Peter I's godchild had become Pyotr Petrovich Petrov (Christian name, patronymic, and surname), but he had grown used in Turkey to the name of Ibrahim and was allowed to call himself by its Russian counterpart, Avraam or Abram. Actually, he should not have boggled at bearing his godfather's name: after all, it had been a Petrus Aethiops (Pasfa Sayon Malbazo) who published in Rome, about 1549, after thirteen years of labor, the New Testament in the language of Abyssinian liturgy (that is, Geez, the ancient Ethiopic, which was later replaced by Amharic).

The statement in the beginning of the German biography to the effect that Abram's father, a proud Abyssinian seigneur, traced his lineage two thousand years back to Hannibal, the famous Carthaginian general, is of course nonsense: it is impossible to conceive that an Abyssinian of the seventeenth century should have known anything of him. The surname Gannibal was applied to Abram in official documents as early as 1723, upon his return from France. In other references, and in all earlier ones, he is called *Abram arap* or *Abram Petrov Arap*, where the middle term is the patronymic in the act of changing into a surname. It is interesting to mark how puzzled Russian commentators are by this choice of name, which in reality is such an obvious one. Anuchin, for example, absurdly suggests that Abram or Abram's family might have derived "Gannibal" from Adi Baro (a village just north of Debarwa, northern Abyssinia)! Why not from Lalibala (an Abyssinian emperor of the thirteenth century), or from Hamalmal (a provincial governor who rebelled against his royal cousin, Malak Sagad I, in the late 1500's), or, still better, from *gane bal*, which means "strange master" in Tigré; there are no holds barred in these linguistic *petits-jeux*.

Actually, of course, our hero's eponym was as trite and familiar a figure in the pseudoclassically minded Europe of the eighteenth century—in its textbooks, essays, historical works, newspaper articles, and academic speeches—as were Caesar and Cicero. In Tsar Peter's Russia no illumination was complete without the names of Greek and Roman heroes appearing in a pyrotechnical display of old saws. Pushkin was quite right in Gallicizing the adopted surname that Abram had most probably brought from France in 1723. There, and in Italy, it was not infrequently met with as a given name (e.g., François Annibal, duc d'Estrées, d. 1687). He had certainly encountered it in his military studies. He had read about "le grand génie d'Annibal" in Bossuet's *Discours sur l'histoire universelle*. If he really took part in the Spanish War, he must have been stationed in 1719 at the fort of Bellegarde (rebuilt by Vauban in 1679) and have trodden there, on the Spanish border, near the village of Le Perthus (Pyrénées Orientales), the Elephant Steps of Hannibal's Highway, still visible today among the arbutus and oak brush. And one also wonders if in Metz he had not had for schoolmate a certain Pierre Robert *dit* Annibal (1699–1783), who must have been living there about 1720, according to the parish records published by Poirier.

### GANNIBAL'S LATER YEARS IN RUSSIA (1723–81)

*Le capitaine Petrov dit Annibal*, having acquired in France some knowledge of bulwarks and buttresses, lived, from 1723 on, in Russia, teaching mathematics and building fortresses. I have not performed any special research in regard to this final lap of his life; it is fairly well known in its main features, and, as Russian commentators have pointed out, Pushkin's presentation of Abram's Siberian period is false. On May 8, 1727, im-

mediately after the end of Catherine I's reign, he was
dispatched to inspect a fort in Kazan and then to build
one in Selenginsk, on the Chinese border—where,
incidentally, Lieutenant Gannibal encountered his former patron, Count Vladislavich-Raguzinski, who was
returning from his Chinese embassy. Vaguely accused
of political intrigue, Gannibal found himself kept at
work in Selenginsk and Tobolsk for a couple of years,
and only in the beginning of Anna's reign the governor
of St. Petersburg, Münnich, needing a good military
engineer, had him transferred to a Baltic fort. In 1731,
Gannibal married Evdokia (Eudoxia) Dioper, daughter
of a sea captain, Andrey Dioper, presumably of Greek
origin. She was unfaithful to him, and so was he to her.
According to documents described by Stepan Opatovich
(in *Russkaya starina*, 1877), Gannibal, in 1732, rigged
up at his home a private torture chamber complete with
pulleys, iron clamps, thumbkins, leathern whips, and so
forth. An obstinate and formalistic man, he then managed
to have his victim imprisoned by the state for marital
betrayal. She stayed five years in jail, after which—while
divorce proceedings were dragging on—she was more
or less at liberty till 1753, when the final separation was
accorded; upon which, the unfortunate woman was
packed away to a remote convent, where she died. In
the meantime, in 1736, Gannibal had married (unlaw-
fully) his mistress of four years' standing, the daughter
of another captain, an army captain this time, named
Matthias Schöberg, Lutheran, of Swedish-German
descent. By this second wife (whose first name was
Christina Regine, according to the German biography)
Gannibal had eleven children, of whom the third son,
Osip, was to be Pushkin's maternal grandfather.

Gannibal spent a few years as a country squire on a
piece of acquired land, and then went on building fortresses. In 1742, Elizabeth, Peter I's younger daughter,

made him a major general and four years later granted him the countryseat Mihaylovskoe in the province of Pskov, which was to be forever linked up with Pushkin's name. During these years, Gannibal proved himself an expert at arranging fireworks at state festivals and composing denunciations of various officials. In 1762, after building his last fortress and propelling his last rocket, he was retired and lived in obscure senility for another twenty years on yet another country estate (Suida, near Petersburg), where he died in 1781, at the advanced age of (probably) eighty-eight.

### CONCLUSIONS

Besides the unfinished romance (1827) "*The Blackamoor of Peter the Great*" (in which a greatly glamorized Ibrahim is given fictitious adventures in France and Russia—all this not in the author's best vein), there is among Pushkin's works a remarkable piece in verse referring to the same character. In this postscriptum of five stanzas to a poem on his paternal lineage (*Moya rodoslovnaya*), in iambic tetrameter, Pushkin has this to say about his maternal ancestor (I have not rendered the rhymes, feminine and masculine, which alternate in the original):

> Figlyarin, snug at home, decided
> That my black grandsire, Gannibal,
> Was for a bottle of rum acquired
> And fell into a skipper's hands.

> This skipper was the glorious skipper
> Through whom our country was advanced,
> Who to our native vessel's helm
> Gave mightily a sovereign course.

> This skipper was accessible
> To my grandsire; the blackamoor,
> Bought at a bargain, grew up stanch and loyal,
> The emperor's bosom friend, not slave.

"Figlyarin" (from *figlyar*, a zany, a coarse buffoon) is a play on the name of a hated reviewer, Fadey (Thaddeus, Thady) Bulgarin. It was thought up by the minor poet Vyazemski, Pushkin's friend, and first used by another poet, Baratïnski, in a published epigram of 1827. Pushkin's piece was written on Oct. 16, 1830, and revised on Dec. 3 of the same year. It is his answer (posthumously published in 1846) to the following vicious innuendo by Bulgarin in his magazine *Severnaya pchela* (The Northern Bee), no. 94 (Aug. 7, 1830):

Byron's lordship [*lordstvo*] and aristocratic capers, combined with God knows what way of thinking, have driven to frenzy a multitude of poets and rhymesters in various countries: all of them have started talking about their six-hundred-year-old nobility! . . . It is openly related that some poet or other in Spanish America, likewise an imitator of Byron, being of mulatto descent on his father's or (I do not quite remember) mother's side, began to affirm that one of his ancestors was a Negro prince. A search in the town hall's archives disclosed that in the past there had been a lawsuit between a skipper and his mate on account of that Negro, and that the skipper maintained he had acquired the Negro for a bottle of rum.

And Nikolay Grech adds in his memoirs (*Zapiski moey zhizni*, St. Petersburg, 1886, p. 456) that the story of the transaction supposedly made in Kronstadt was first told by Count S. Uvarov at the Olenins'.

It would be a waste of time to conjecture that Abram was not born in Abyssinia at all; that he had been captured by slave traders in a totally different place—say, the Lagona region of equatorial Africa, south of Lake Chad, inhabited by Mussulman Negroes; or that he was, as Helbig (1809) affirms, a homeless little *Mohr* (Negro), acquired in Holland by Peter I to serve as a ship's boy (Bulgarin's source); we may also brood on the puzzling question why Gannibal, with his sense of the political, and Pushkin, with his sense of the exotic, never once allude to Abyssinia (Pushkin, of course, knew of its mention in the German biography, the Russian translation of which had been dictated to him). Nonetheless, it is upon nonbelievers in the Abyssinian theory that the burden of the proof rests; while, on the other hand, those who accept it must waver between seeing in Pushkin the great-great-grandson of one of those rude and free Negro nomads who haunted the Mareb region or a descendant of Solomon and the Queen of Sheba, from whom Abyssinian kings derived their dynasty.

According to N. Barsukov (1891), who had it from Elizaveta Pushkin, widow of our poet's brother Lev, the hands of Nadezhda Gannibal, Pushkin's mother, had yellowish palms; and according to another source, quoted by V. Vinogradov (1930), all the daughters of Isaak Gannibal, Pushkin's grand-uncle, son of Abram, spoke with a peculiar singsong intonation—"an African accent," quaintly says an old-timer, who remarks that they "cooed like Egyptian pigeons." There exists no authentic portrait of Abram Gannibal. A late eighteenth-century oil, which some suppose represents him, wearing a decoration he never received, is, anyway, hopelessly stylized by the dauber. Nor can one draw any conclusion from the portraits of his progeny as to what blood predominated in Abram, Negro or Caucasian. In Pushkin, admixtures of Slavic and German strains must have completely obscured whatever definite racial characteristics his ancestors may have possessed, while the fact that certain portraits of Pushkin by good artists, and his death mask, do bear a remarkable resemblance to modern photographs of typical Abyssinians is exactly what one might expect in the descendant of a Negro married to a Caucasian. It should be repeated that "Abyssinian" implies a very complicated blend of the Hamitic and the Semitic and that, moreover, distinct Negroid types commingle with Caucasian ones on the northern plateau and among ruling families almost as much as they do among the nomadic heathens of the lowland brush. The Galla tribes (the Oromota), for example, who overran the country simultaneously with the Turkish invasion in the sixteenth century, are Hamites with a strong Negro strain. Abram may have had the characteristics that Bent found in the Tigré and Hamasen tribes: "skin . . . of a rich chocolate color, the hair curly, the nose straight with a tendency toward the aquiline, the lips thickish," or—while still technically an Abyssinian—he might have possessed the traits that Pushkin, a conventionalist in these matters, gives Ibrahim in his novel: "a black skin, a flat nose, inverted lips, and rough woolly hair" (ch. 5). The taxonomic problem remains unsettled and will probably remain so despite "anthropological sketches" of the Anuchin brand. And although Abram Gannibal used to refer to himself, in humble letters to grandees, as "a poor Negro," and although Pushkin saw him as a Negro with "African passions" and an independent brilliant personality, actually Pyotr Petrovich Petrov, alias Abram Gannibal, was a sour, groveling, crotchety, timid, ambitious, and cruel person; a good military engineer, perhaps, but humanistically a nonentity; differing in nothing from a typical career-minded, superficially educated, coarse, wife-flogging Russian of his day, in a brutal and dull world of political intrigue, favoritism, Germanic regimentation, old-fashioned Russian misery, and fat-breasted empresses on despicable thrones.

Basing himself on the fact that in 1899, under Italian domination, Debarwa, once the capital of Tigré, was included in a district called at that time "Logon-Chuan" (an assemblage of letters I have been unable to check), Anuchin comes to the singular conclusion, for which there is not a scrap of evidence, that two centuries earlier Logo was synonymous with Debarwa. In Poncet's day (summer, 1700), Debarwa was divided into two towns, upper and lower, the lower one being assigned to Mohammedans; in Bruce's time, seventy years later, not Debarwa but Adowa, a neighboring town, was the capital of Tigré; and by the end of the nineteenth century, Debarwa was "a place of abject squalor and misery" (Bent, 1893). But if Anuchin is right in identifying "L" with Logo or Legota, it is in that general district that clues should be sought today; for there may still persist a faint chance of experts in Abyssinian history and lore discovering on the spot some trace, some memory, of the circumstances and events that resulted in the son of an Abyssinian becoming a Russian general in the eighteenth century.

We shall now go back to a certain passage in Pushkin's note to One : L : 11, in the separate edition of Chapter One of *EO* (1825). It reads:

Up to an advanced age, Annibal still remembered Africa, the luxurious life of his father, and nineteen brothers, of whom he was the youngest; he remembered how they used to be led into his father's presence with their hands bound behind their backs, whilst he alone remained free and went swimming under the fountains of the paternal home . . .

Had Pushkin explicitly stated here that the paternal home was in Abyssinia, we might have argued that he had borrowed from literary sources of his time this strikingly specific detail of an Ethiopian ruler's sons being treated as captives, potential parricides, possible usurpers. The banishment of young princes to bleak hilltops in the Tigré Province by kings and viceroys as a precaution against violent succession had had a great romanesque impact on the imagination of western Europe in the eighteenth century. And, most curiously, the Abyssinian chronicler Za-Ouald (French transcription) tells us that in the twenty-second year (1702, 1703, or 1704) of Jesus I's reign he caused all his sons to be put in chains—and was assassinated a couple of years later by his only free son, Tekla. I do not think that Pushkin deliberately introduced here this local note—to corroborate a statement of locus he had never made and allude to a specific incident he could not have known. It seems more plausible to suppose that the governor of "L" dutifully followed his "sultan" in this colorful custom. In fact, I would say that this, and the sister's name Lahann, are the only details that have a true Abyssinian flavor.

The other detail, concerning the swimming under the fountains, *pod fontanami*, is less convincing, unless we take it to imply cascades, small waterfalls, etc., and not the playing sprays of an African Versailles, Abram's paternal home. Of that home we know even less than we do of a certain farm at Snitterfield, near Stratford. One thinks of the faucets in Johnson's watery *Rasselas* (of which Salt thought in Abyssinia) as well as of the *cent mille jets d'eau* of King Belus' marble palace on the Euphrates in Voltaire's unreadable novella *Voyages et Aventures d'une princesse babylonienne, pour servir de suite à ceux de Scarmentado, par un vieux philosophe qui ne radote pas toujours* (Geneva, 1768): ". . . Chacun sait comme le roi d'Éthiopie devint amoureux de la belle Formonsante" (daughter of Belus, king of Babylon) "[et] qu'Amazan" (her lover) ". . . coupa la tête perverse du nègre insolent." Kammerer (1949), pl. cxII, reproduces the picture of "le Roi d'Éthiopie abusant de son pouvoir" (embracing a distraught pale-skinned lady in her bed), which is a vignette by Monnet, engraved by Vidal, in Bevillon's edition (Paris, 1778) of Voltaire's *Romans et contes*.

If one likes to think that Dr. Johnson's contemporary, Pushkin's great-grandfather, was born practically in "Rasselas'" lap, at the foot of the joint memorial blend-

ing Ethiopian history and the didactic romance of the
French eighteenth century, one may allow oneself also
to visualize a Frenchman of Louis XIV's time feasting
with Pushkin's dusky great-great-grandfather in the
land of Prester John. Let me conclude these rapid notes
about Gannibal with the following poetical excerpt from
the anonymous English translation (1709) of the travels
of Charles Poncet, who stayed in Debarwa in the summer
of 1700 (pp. 149–50):

After a solemn service for the emperor's son [Fasilidas,
heir to the throne], who had just died, the two Governors
[*les deux Barnagas*] seated themselves in a great hall, and
placed me in the middle between 'em. After that, the
officers and persons of note, both men and women, rang'd
themselves round the hall. Certain women with tabors
[*tambours de basque*] . . . began to sing [*commencèrent
des récits en forme de chansons*] . . . in so doleful a tone
that I could not hinder being seized with grief. . . .

One's marginal imagination conjures up here many
a pleasing possibility. We recall Coleridge's Abyssinian
maid (*Kubla Khan*, 1797) singing of "Mount Abora,"
which (unless it merely echoes the name of the musical
instrument) is, I suggest, either Mt. Tabor, an amba
(natural citadel), some 3000 feet high in the Siré district
of the Tigré, or still more exactly the unlocated amba
Abora, which I find mentioned by the chronicler Za-
Ouald (in Basset's translation) as being the burial place
of a certain high official named Gyorgis (one of Poncet's
two governors?) in 1707. We may further imagine that
Coleridge's and Poncet's doleful singer was none other
than Pushkin's great-great-grandmother; that her lord,
either of Poncet's two hosts, was Pushkin's great-great-
grandfather; and that the latter was a son of Cella
Christos, Dr. Johnson's Rasselas. There is nothing in
the annals of Russian Pushkinology to restrain one from
the elaboration of such fancies.

## Works Consulted

ABBADIE, ANTOINE D', and PAULITSCHKE, PHILIPPE [PHILIPP], trs. *Des Conquêtes faites en Abyssinie en XVI^e siècle par l'Imam Muhammad Ahmad dit Grâgne* [Gran or Gaurane]; *version française de la chronique arabe* [for the years 1523–35] *Futûh el-Hábacha* [of Aḥmad ibn 'Abd al-Kādir ibn Salīm ibn 'Uthmān]. Paris, 1898.

ALMEIDA, MANOEL DE. See BECKINGHAM, C. F., and HUNTINGFORD, G. W. B., trs. and eds. *Some Records of Ethiopia*.

ANUCHIN, DMITRI. "A. S. Pushkin. Antropologicheskiy eskiz" (A. S. Pushkin. An Anthropological Sketch), *Russkie vedomosti* (Russian Gazette; Moscow), nos. 99, 106, 120, 127, 134, 143, 172, 180, 193, 209 (Apr. 10–July 31, 1899). A very poor and misleading work.

ARMBRUSTER, CHARLES HUBERT. *Initia Amharica*. Pt. III: *Amharic-English Vocabulary*. Cambridge, 1920.

BANTÏSH-KAMENSKI, DMITRI. *Slovar' dostopamyatnïh lyudey Russkoy zemli* (Dictionary of Distinguished Russians). Moscow, 1836. 5 vols.

BARATIERI, ORESTE. *Mémoires d'Afrique (1892–1896)*. Paris, 1899. Map: "Carta generale della colonia Eritrea" (1 : 1,000,000).

BASSET, RENÉ. "Études sur l'histoire d'Éthiopie," *Journal asiatique* (Paris), 7th ser., XVII (1881), 315–434; XVIII (1881), 93–183, 285–389. Contains (XVIII, 293–324) a "Chronique éthiopienne" (a French translation of the chronicle of the reign of Jesus I) begun by the imperial secretary Haouâryâ Krestos (French transliteration), killed in battle in 1698, and continued by the next secretary, Za-Ouald (Fr.).

BECKINGHAM, C. F., and HUNTINGFORD, G. W. B., trs. and eds. *Some Records of Ethiopia, 1593–1646; Being Extracts from The History of High Ethiopia or Abassia, by Manoel de Almeida, together with Bahrey's History of the Galla*. London, 1954. (Works Issued by the Hakluyt Society, 2nd ser., CVII.)

BÉGIN, ÉMILE AUGUSTE. *Histoire des sciences, des lettres, des arts et de la civilisation dans le pays Messin*. Metz, 1829.

BENT, J. THEODORE. *The Sacred City of the Ethiopians, Being a Record of Travel and Research in Abyssinia in 1893*. London, 1893. Maps.

BOGOSLOVSKI, M. *Pyotr I. Materialï dlya biografii* (Peter I.

Materials for a Biography). Leningrad, 1940–48. 5 vols.

BONNAC, JEAN LOUIS DUSSON, MARQUIS DE. *Mémoire historique sur l'ambassade de France à Constantinople* (early eighteenth century), ed. Charles Schefer. Paris, 1894. Contains (pp. 113–33) "Mémoire de Monsieur de Ferriol pour rendre compte de son ambassade" (to the Ottoman Porte, Dec. 25, 1699, to 1708).

BRUCE, JAMES. *Travels to Discover the Source of the Nile in the Years 1768, 1769, 1771, 1772 and 1773.* Edinburgh, 1790. 5 vols. Maps.

BUDGE, SIR E. A. WALLIS. *A History of Ethiopia.* London, 1928. 2 vols.

BURTON, SIR RICHARD F. *First Footsteps in East Africa; or, An Exploration of Harar.* London, 1856.

BUVAT, JEAN. *Journal de la Régence (1715–1723)*, ed. Émile Campardon. Paris, 1865. 2 vols.

CASTANHOSO, MIGUEL DE. See WHITEWAY, R. S., tr. and ed. *The Portuguese Expedition to Abyssinia in 1541–1543.*

DANGEAU, PHILIPPE DE COURCILLON, MARQUIS DE. *Journal*, ed. E. Soulié, L. E. Dussieux, P. de Chennevières, P. Mantz, A. de Montaiglon, avec les additions du duc de Saint-Simon. Paris, 1854–60. 19 vols. Vol. XVII (1717–19).

*Encyclopaedia of Islam*, ed. M. Th. Houtsma, A. J. Wensinck, et al. Leiden and London, 1911–38. 4 vols. in 8.

FOSTER, SIR WILLIAM, ed. *The Red Sea and Adjacent Countries at the Close of the Seventeenth Century, as Described by Joseph Pitts, William Daniel, and Charles Jacques Poncet.* London, 1949. (Works Issued by the Hakluyt Society, 2nd ser., C.)

*Gallereya Petra Velikogo v imperatorskoy publichnoy biblioteke* (Gallery of Peter the Great in the Imperial Public Library). St. Petersburg, 1903.

GANNIBAL, ANNA. "Gannibalï. Novïe dannïe dlya ih biografiy" (The Gannibals. New Data for Their Biography), pt. I. In *Pushkin i ego sovremenniki* (Pushkin and His Contemporaries; Petrograd), V, 17–18 (1914), 205–48. Pt. II (Catalogue of Abram Gannibal's Library) in ibid., V, 19–20 (1914), 270–309.

GASTFREYND, N. "Pis'ma Abraama Gannibala" (Abram Gannibal's Letters), *Vsemirnïy vestnik* (International Messenger; St. Petersburg), XI (1903); separate edition, 1904 (fide Vegner).

GOBAT, SAMUEL. *Journal of Three Years' Residence in Abyssinia*, tr. Sereno D. Clark. New York, 1851. Map (evidently copied from Salt).

GOFMAN, M., ed. "Dnevnik A. N. Vulfa. 1828–1831" (Journal of A. N. Vulf. 1828–1831). In *Pushkin i ego sovremenniki* (Pushkin and His Contemporaries; Petrograd), VI, 21–22 (1915), 1–310.

GOLIKOV, IVAN. *Anekdotï, kasayushchiesya do Petra V.* (sic) (Anecdotes Concerning Peter the Great). Moscow, 1798.

———. *Deyaniya Petra Velikogo, mudrogo preobrazïtelya Rossii, sobrannïe iz dostovernïh istochnikov i raspolozhennïe po godam.* (Acts of Peter the Great, Compiled from Authentic Sources and Arranged Chronologically.) 1st edn., Moscow, 1788–89; 2nd edn., Moscow, 1837–43. 15 vols.

HAMMER-PURGSTALL, JOSEPH VON. *Histoire de l'Empire ottoman depuis son origine jusqu'à nos jours*, tr. (from German) J. J. Hellert. Paris, 1835–43. 18 vols. Vol. XIII (1699–1718).

HARRIS, MAJOR W. CORNWALLIS. *The Highlands of Aethiopia.* London, 1844. 3 vols.

HELBIG, H. VON. *Russische Günstlinge*. Tübingen, 1809 (written 1787?). Russian tr. in *Russkaya starina* (Russian Antiquity; St. Petersburg), L (1886), 14–180.

HERVEZ, JEAN. *La Régence galante: Les Chroniques du XVIII$^e$ siècle.* Paris, 1909.

JOHNSON, SAMUEL. *The Prince of Abissinia (The History of Rasselas, Prince of Abissinia,* in later edns.). London, 1759. Russian version: *Rasselas, prints abissinskiy.* Moscow, 1795.

JONES, A. H. M., and MONROE, ELIZABETH. *A History of Abyssinia.* Oxford, 1935.

KAMMERER, ALBERT. *La mer Rouge, l'Abyssinie et l'Arabie depuis l'antiquité.* Cairo, 1929–52. 3 vols. in 7. Vol. III: *La mer Rouge, l'Abyssinie et l'Arabie au XVI$^e$ et XVII$^e$ siècles et la cartographie des Portulans du monde oriental.* Pt. I: "XVI$^e$ siècle. Abyssins et Portugais devant l'Islam." Pt. II: "XVII$^e$ siècle. Les Jésuites portugais et l'ephémère triomphe du catholicisme en Abyssinie (1603–1632)." Pt. III: "La Cartographie du monde oriental, mer Rouge, océan Indien et Extrême-Orient jusqu'au XVIII$^e$ siècle. Cartographes portugais et français."

KORB, JOHANN GEORG. *Diary of an Austrian Secretary of*

*Legation at the Court of Czar Peter the Great*, tr. (from Latin; Vienna, 1700) Count Charles MacDonnell. London, 1863. 2 vols.

LECLERCQ, HENRI. *Histoire de la Régence pendant la minorité de Louis XV*. Paris, 1921. 3 vols. Vol. I, ch. 17.

LEFEBVRE, THÉOPHILE; PETIT, A.; QUARTIN-DILLON, R., and VIGNAUD. *Voyage en Abyssinie exécuté pendant les années 1839, 1840, 1841, 1842, 1843*. Paris, 1845–51. 6 vols. Pt. I (vols. I, II): "Relation historique," by Lefebvre. Pt. II (vol. III): "Itinéraire," etc., by Lefebvre.

LE GRAND or LEGRAND, JOACHIM. *Voyage historique d'Abissinie, du R.P. Jérôme Lobo de la Compagnie de Jésus*, traduite du Portugais, continuée et augmentée de plusieurs dissertations, lettres et mémoires. Paris and La Haye, 1728.

LONGINOV, MIHAIL. "Abram Petrovich Gannibal," *Russkiy arhiv* (Russian Archive; Moscow), II (1864), 218–32.

LUDOLF, JOB (HIOB LEUTHOLF). *Historia aethiopica*. Frankfort, 1681. And the commentary to it (*Ad suam Historiam aethiopicam antehac editam commentarius*). Frankfort, 1691. (Seen in quotations and in a French version.) His map (in Kammerer) was made from the accounts of Portuguese Jesuits and pub. 1684 in the 2nd edn. of the English tr. of the *Historia*. It was engraved as late as 1728 for Le Grand's edn. of Father Lobo's narrative.

MARAIS, MATHIEU. *Journal de Paris, 1721–1723*. In *Revue rétrospective; ou, Bibliothèque historique* (Paris), 2nd ser., VII–IX (1836–37).

MATHEW, DAVID. *Ethiopia: The Study of a Polity, 1540–1935*. London, 1947.

MODZALEVSKI, B. "Rod Pushkina" (Pushkin's Ancestry). In S. Vengerov's edn. of Pushkin's works, vol. I, St. Petersburg, 1907. Posthumously repub. with some corrections, Leningrad, 1929.

MUNZINGER, WERNER. *Vocabulaire de la langue tigré*. Leipzig, 1865.

OLDEROGGE, D., ed. *Abissiniya (Efiopiya). Sbornik statey* (Collected Papers). Moscow and Leningrad, 1936. Of little interest.

OPATOVICH, S. "Evdokiya Andreevna Gannibal, pervaya zhena Abraama Petrovicha Gannibala. 1731–1753" (Evdokiya Andreevna Gannibal, Abram Gannibal's First Wife), *Russkaya starina* (Russian Antiquity; St. Petersburg), XVIII (1877), 69–78.

PEKARSKI, PYOTR. *Nauka i literatura v Rossii pri Petre Velikom* (Russian Science and Literature in the Era of Peter the Great). St. Petersburg, 1862. 2 vols. (Vol. I seen in excerpts.)

PERRUCHON, JULES. "Notes pour l'histoire d'Éthiopie: Le règne de Iyasu (I$^{er}$), roi d'Éthiopie de 1682 à 1706," *Revue sémitique* (Paris), IX (1901), 161–67.

PETER I. *Pis'ma i bumagi imperatora Petra Velikogo* (Letters and Documents of Emperor Peter the Great). Vols. V and VI. St. Petersburg, 1907 and 1912.

——. *Zhurnal ili podyonnaya zapiska* (Journal or Diary). Pt. I (1698–1714). St. Petersburg, 1770.

——. See also *Gallereya Petra Velikogo*.

PEZHEMSKI, PYOTR. "Panorama Irkutskoy gubernii" (Panorama of the Province of Irkutsk), pt. II, *Sovremennik* (The Contemporary; St. Petersburg), XXII (1850), 1–38.

PIOSSENS, CHEVALIER DE. *Mémoires de la Régence*. Paris, 1749. 5 vols. Vol. II.

POIRIER, ABBÉ F. J. *Metz. Documents généalogiques, 1561–1792*. Paris, 1899.

PONCET, CHARLES. *Relation abrégée du voyage que M. Charles Poncet fit en Éthiopie en 1698, 1699 et 1700*. In *Lettres édifiantes et curieuses, écrites des missions étrangères, par quelques missionaires de la C$^{ie}$ de Jésus*. Vol. IV, pp. 251–443. Paris, 1713. English version: *A Voyage to Aethiopia, Made in the Years 1698, 1699, and 1700*, tr. anon. (from the French of a lost 1st edn., 1704, of Poncet's account). London, 1709.

——. See also FOSTER, SIR WILLIAM, ed. *The Red Sea and Adjacent Countries*.

PUSHKIN, ALEKSANDR. *Polnoye sobranie sochineniy* (Complete Works). Akademiya nauk, Leningrad, 1937–50, 1959. 17 vols. in 20.

——. *Rukoyu Pushkina. Nesobrannïe i neopublikovannïe tekstï* (By Pushkin's Hand. Uncompiled and Uncollected Texts), ed. and annot. M. Tsyavlovski, L. Modzalevski, and T. Zenger. Leningrad, 1935. "Biografiya A. P. Gannibala," pp. 34–59. German text of biography, pp. 43–49; first published; annot. by Zenger.

*Russkiy biograficheskiy slovar'* (Russian Biographical Dictionary). St. Petersburg, 1896–1913. Set seen has 25 vols., with "V" and "M" missing.

SALT, HENRY. "Mr. Salt's Narrative." In Valentia, George, Viscount. *Voyages and Travels to India, Ceylon, the Red Sea, Abyssinia and Egypt.* 4 vols. London, 1811. Vol. II, pp. 421–89; vol. III, pp. 1–249.

——. *A Voyage to Abyssinia and Travels into the Interior of That Country, Executed under the Orders of the British Government in the Years 1809 and 1810.* London, 1814. Another edn., Philadelphia, 1816. With a map of Abyssinia (not present in the Cornell University library copy of the 1814 edn.).

SHMURLO, E. "Gannibal." In Brokgauz [Brockhaus] and Efron *Entsiklopedicheskiy slovar'* (Encyclopedia). Vol. VIII. St. Petersburg, 1892.

STARKIE, ENID. *Arthur Rimbaud in Abyssinia.* Oxford, 1937.

SUMNER, B. H. *Peter the Great and the Ottoman Empire.* Oxford, 1949.

TURAEV, B., tr. *Abissinskie hroniki XIV–XVI vv.* (Abyssinian Chronicles of the XIV–XVI Centuries), tr. from Ethiopian. Moscow and Leningrad, 1936.

U. S. ARMY MAP SERVICE. *Asmara* (1 : 1,000,000). No. 100052. Washington, D. C., Feb., 1943.

USTRYALOV, N. *Istoriya tsarstvovaniya Petra Velikogo* (A History of the Reign of Peter the Great). Vol. III, St. Petersburg, 1858; vol. IV, pts. 1 and 2 (Appendixes), bound separately, St. Petersburg, 1863.

VALENTIA, GEORGE, VISCOUNT. *Voyages and Travels to . . . Abyssinia . . .* See SALT, HENRY. "Mr. Salt's Narrative."

VEGNER, M. *Predki Pushkina* (Pushkin's Ancestors). [Moscow], 1937. A very poor compilation.

VINOGRADOV, L.; CHULKOV, N., and ROSANOV, N. *A. S. Pushkin v Moskve. Sbornik statey* (A. S. Pushkin in Moscow. Collected Papers). Moscow, 1930. (Trudï Obschestva Moskovskoy oblasti VII.)

VULF, ALEKSEY. See GOFMAN, M., ed. "Dnevnik A. N. Vulfa. 1828–1831."

WHITEWAY, R. S., tr. and ed. *The Portuguese Expedition to Abyssinia in 1541–1543, as Narrated by Castanhoso.* London, 1902. (Works Issued by the Hakluyt Society, 2nd ser., X.)

*Index*

# A

Abbadie, Antoine d': *Des Conquêtes faites en Abyssinie*, 162
Abha, 121
*Abissinya, see* Olderogge
*Abissinskie hroniki, see* Turaev
Abora (amba), 161
Abram arap / Petrov arap, *see* Gannibal, A. P.
Abyssinia / -ian (Ethiopia), 118–34, 135, 137n, 143, 144, 147, 152, 156, 157–61
Abyssinian Church, 128
Acosta / Dekosta, Jan d', 146 & n
*Acts of Peter the Great, see* Golikov: *Deyaniya*
Adi Baro, 152
Adowa, 159
Adyam, *see* Jesus I
Africa / -an, 108, 109, 116, 117, 118, 132, 144, 156, 157, 158, 159, 160
Ahmad ibn . . . 'Uthmān, 162
Ahmed III, sultan of Turkey, 137, 138, 141
Ahmed Pasha ("Beehive"), 138
Aisne, 149
Aksum, 123, 127, 129
Aleksandronevskiy Monastery / -tïr', 151
Aleksey Petrovich, tsarevich, *see* Alexis, Prince
Alexandria, 127
Alexis, Prince (s. of Peter I), 138–9
Ali Pasha, 138
Almeida, Manoel de, 120, 124, 130n, 162
Amazan, 160; *see also* Arouet: *Voyages*
America, 151
Amharic, 127, 152
*Anecdotes, see* Scherer
"Anekdot," *see* Bulgarin
*Anekdoti, see* Gilokov
Angiolo, Jacopo d' (Angola della Scarperia), 120

Anna Ivanovna / Ioannovna, empress, 110 & n, 154
Anna Leopoldovna, empress, 110n
Annenkov, P. V., *see* P., PUSHKINIANA: *Pushkin*
Annesley Bay, 121
Annibal, A. P., *see* Gannibal, A. P.
Annibal, I. A., *see* Gannibal, I. A.
"Annibal," Pierre Robert, 153
Antalo, 124
Anuchin, Dmitri Nikolaevich, 118, 119, 120, 121, 129, 152, 158, 159
Anville, Jean Baptiste Bourguignon d', 120
Arab / -ia / -ic, 117, 126n, 127, 132, 135, 141 & n, 147
"Arab Petra Velikogo," *see* P., WORKS
Armbruster, C. H.: *Initia Amharica*, 162
Armenia, 132
Arouet, François Marie ("Voltaire"), 150; *Romans et contes*, 123, 160; *Voyages et aventures d'une princesse babylonienne*, 160
Asmara, 124, 130n
Atbara, 121
Athanasius, 127
Augustus II, king of Poland, 144
Austria, 136n, 138
Azov, 138, 142

# B

Bahafa, king of Abyssinia, 127
Bahrey / Bahri: *History of the Galla*, 162
Ballantyne's Novelist's Library, 122n
Baltaji, Mohammed, 138
Baltic Region / Sea, 154

Bantïsh-Kamenski, D. N., 114;
*Slovar' dostopamyatnïh lyu-
dey Russkoy zemli* (Dictionary of Distinguished People of
the Russian Land), 162
Barataria (in Cervantes), 145
Baratieri, Oreste, 124; *Mém-
oires d'Afrique*, 162
Baratïnski, Evgeniy Abramo-
vich, 156
Baruskov, N. P., 157
Basset, René, 127, 129, 130,
131, 161, 162
Beckingham, C. F., and Hun-
tingford, G. W. B., 123, 129,
130; *Some Records of Ethi-
opia*, 162
Bégin, Emile Auguste, 149;
*Histoire . . . de la civilisation
dans le pays Messin*, 162
Belessa River, 121, 122
Belidor, Bernard Forest de,
149; *Sommaire d'un cours
d'architecture militaire*, 149
Bellegarde, fort de, 153
Belus, King, 160; *see also*
Arouet: *Voyages*
Bent, J. Theodore, 121, 158,
159; *Sacred City of the Ethi-
opians, The*, 162
Bevillon, 160
*Biografiya A. P. Gannibala*
(anon.), *see* Gannibal, Abram,
German biography of
Biron / Bühren, Ernst Johann,
110 & n
Bizan / Bizen, *see* Debra
"Blackamoor of Peter the
Great," *see* P., works: "Arap
Petra Velikogo"
Black Sea / Chyornoe More /
Pontus Euxinus, 107n
Bogoslovski, M. M.: *Pyotr I*,
142–5
Bondi, S. M., *see* P., push-
kiniana: *Works*
Bonnac, Jean Louis Dusson,
Marquis de, 137n; *Mémoire*

historique sur l'ambassade de
France à Constantinople, 163
Bosnia, 141
Bossuet, Jacques Bénigne, 151;
*Discours sur l'histoire univer-
selle*, 153
Brockhaus / Russ. Brokgauz,
and Efron, 167; *see also* P.,
pushkiniana: *Works* (ed. Ven-
gerov)
Bruce, James (traveler), 120,
124, 128, 134, 159; *Travels*,
131–2, 163
Budge, Sir E. A. Wallis, 130,
131; *History of Ethiopia, A*,
163
Bug River, 137n
Bühren, *see* Biron
Bulaq, 134
Bulgarin, Fadey / Faddey Ven-
ediktovich, 156; "Byron's
lordship," 156
Burton, Sir Richard F.: *First
Footsteps in East Africa*, 163
Buvat, Jean: *Journal de la
Régence*, 163
Byron / Russ. Bayron, George
Gordon, Baron, 156

## C

Caesar, Gaius Julius, 153
Cairo, 132, 133, 134
Carthage, 152
Cashaat, 122
Castanhoso, Miguel de, 163,
167
Catalonia, 149
Catherine I, empress, 110n,
139, 154
Catherine II, empress, 110 & n,
111
Caucasian race, 116, 117, 157
Chad, Lake, 156
Champière Island, 149
Chardin, Jean, 151
Chateaubriand, Viscount Fran-
çois René de, 151

Chennevières, P. de, 163
China / -ese, 145, 154
Christian / -ity / -ize, 127–8, 131, 132, 134, 138, 142, 144
Christina Eberhardina, queen of Poland, 144
Christos, Cella / Krestos, Ras Ce'ela, 123, 161
Christos, Haouarya, 162
Christos, Keba, 130n
*Chronique éthiopienne* (Krestos and Za-Ouald), 162
Chulkov, N. P., 167
Cicero, Marcus Tullius, 153
Clark, Sereno D., 164
Coleridge, Samuel Taylor: *Kubla Khan*, 161
Constantinople, 109, 115, 116, 117, 118, 134–7, 140, 141 & n, 142, 147, 148
*Contemporary, The*, see *Sovremennik*
Corneille, Pierre, 151
Cornell University Library, 108, 167
Cyrano de Bergerac, Savinien, 151
Cyrillic, 119n

### D

D., Countess Lénore de, 150; *see also* P., WORKS: "Arap Petra Velikogo"
Da Costa, Mendez, 146n
Daltaban the Serbian, 137–8
Dangeau, Philippe de Courcillon, Marquis de: *Journal*, 163
Daniel, William, 163
Debarwa, 121, 123, 128, 129, 130n, 132, 133, 152, 158–9, 161
Debra Bizan / Monastery of Bizen, 130n
Dekosta, Yan, see Acosta
Denmark, 149
*Des Conquêtes faites en Abyssinie*, see Abbadie

Deyaniya Petra Velikogo, see Golikov
*Diary*, see Vulf, Aleksey
*Diary of an Austrian*, see Korb
*Dictionary of Distinguished People*, see Bantïsh-Kamenski: *Slovar'*
Dioper, Andrey, 154
Dioper, Eudoxia / Evdokia, see Gannibal, Eudoxia
*Discours sur l'histoire universelle*, see Bossuet
Dixan, 121, 131
*Dnevnik*, see Vulf, Aleksey
Dobarwa, see Debarwa
Dolgoruki, Prince Vladimir Lukich, 150
Dolgorukov, see Dolgoruki
Dongola, 132
Dunkerque, 148
Dussieux, L. E., 163

### E

Ecole d'Artillerie, see La Fère; Metz
Egypt / Egyptian, 117, 133, 157
Elizaveta Petrovna, empress, 110 & n, 112, 115, 146n, 154–155
*Encyclopaedia of Islam*, 163
Endorta (Tigré-Endorta), 124n, 129, 130, 131
England, 146n
*Entsiklopedicheskiy slovar'* (Brockhaus & Efron Encyclopedia), 167
Estrées, François Annibal, Duke d', 153
Ethiopia, see Abyssinia
*Ethiopia*, see Mathew
*Etudes sur l'histoire d'Ethiopie*, see Basset
*Eugenia owariensis*, 124
Euphrates River, 160
Euxine Sea, see Black Sea

# F

Fares, Ras, 127, 130, 131
Fasilidas (s. of Jesus I), 161
Fasilidas (s. of Susneyos), 128
Figlyarin (=Bulgarin), 155, 156; *see also* Bulgarin
*First Footsteps in East Africa*, *see* Burton
Formosante, 160; *see also* Arouet: *Voyages*
Foster, Sir William: *Red Sea and Adjacent Countries, The*, 163
France / French, 110, 132, 133, 134, 148–51, 152, 153, 155
Franks, 131
Frumentius, 127

# G

Galla (tribe), 130, 158
*Gallereya Petra Velikogo* (Gallery of Peter the Great), 163
Gannibal, (General) Abram / Avram Petrov / Abram Petrovich / Pyotr Petrov (P.'s great-grandfather), 107–67; German biography of (ed. Zenger, in *Rukoyu Pushkina*), 109, 112–19, 123–6, 127, 134–6, 139–40, 144, 145, 147, 149, 151, 152, 157, 166
Gannibal, Anna Semyonovna, 163
Gannibal, Christina (Abram's 2nd wife; P.'s great-grandmother), 111, 113, 154
Gannibal, Eudoxia (daughter of Andrey Dioper; Abram's wife), 154, 165
Gannibal, Isaak Abramovich, 112, 157
Gannibal, Lt. Gen. Ivan Abramovich, 110–11
Gannibal, Maria (daughter of Aleksey Pushkin, m. Osip

Gannibal; P.'s grandmother), 111, 112
Gannibal, Nadezhda (daughter of Osip), *see* Pushkin, Nadezhda
Gannibal, Osip (son of Abram; P.'s grandfather), 111–12, 154
Gannibal, Pyotr Abramovich (P.'s granduncle), 111, 113 & n, 117
Gannibal, Yakov Abramovich, 112
Gastaldi, Jacopo, 120
Gastfreynd, N., 163
"Gaurekos" / Gyorgis / Guirguis, 119, 129–30 & n
Geez language, 130, 152
German, 157
*Geschichte des osmanischen Reiches*, *see* Hammer-Purgstall
Gnacsitares, 151
Gobat, Samuel, 123; *Journal*, 164
Goldsmith, Oliver: *Vicar of Wakefield, The*, 122n
Golikov, I. I., 145; *Anekdotï ... Petra Velikogo* (Anecdotes ... [about] Peter the Great, 164; *Deyaniya Petra Velikogo* (Acts of Peter the Great), 164
Golitsïn, Prince Dmitri Mihaylovich, 137
Golovin, Count Fyodor Alekseevich, 142
Gondar, 129, 132
Gospel, 127
"Gragne" / Gran' / Gran / Gaurane, *see* Muhammad Ahmed
Great Britain, *see* England
Grech, Nikolay Ivanovich, *Zapiski moey zhizni* (Memoirs of My Life), 156; *see also* *Severnaya pchela*
Greek, 153

Greek Catholic / ism / Russ. Pravoslavnïy, 128
Grodno, 143
Guirguis, Asma, 130n
Guirguis, Bahr-negus, *see* "Gaurekos"
Gyorgis, 130, 161

## H

Hamalmal, 152
Hamasen / Hamazen, 119, 120, 127, 158
Hamites, 158
Hamito-Semitic, 116, 157
Hammer-Purgstall, Joseph von, 137n; *Histoire de l'empire ottoman, L'*, 164,
Hannibal / Fr. Annibal / Russ. Gannibal, 117, 152, 153
Hannibal, Awraam Petrowitsch, *see* Gannibal, Abram
Hannibal's Highway, 153
Haraqué (= Gargara?), 125
Harris, W. Cornwallis: *Highlands of Aethiopia*, 164
Harvard University: Houghton Library, 108
Hasan Pasha, 138
Hawaiian Islands, 124n
*Heimkehr, Die, see* Heine
Heine, Heinrich, 126
Helbig, H. von, 114, 156; *Russische Günstlinge*, 164
Hellert, J. J., 164
Hervez, Jean: *Régence galante, La*, 164
Herzegovina, 141
*Highlands of Aethiopia, see* Harris
*Histoire . . . de la civilisation dans le pays Messin, L', see* Bégin
*Histoire de la Régence, L', see* Leclercq
*Histoire de l'empire ottoman, L', see* Hammer-Purgstall
*Historia aethiopica, see* Ludolf

*History of Abyssinia, see* Jones & Monroe
*History of Ethiopia, see* Budge
*History of High Ethiopia or Abassia, see* Beckingham & Huntingford
*History of the Reign of Peter the Great, see* Ustryalov: *Istoriya*
Holland, 146 & n, 148, 156
Houghton Library, *see* Harvard University
Houtsma, M. Th., 163
Hungary, 137n
Huntingford, G. W. B., *see* Beckingham

## I

Ibragim, 114, 141, 155, 158; *see also* P., WORKS: "Arap Petra Velikogo"
Illyria, 141
*Initia Amharica, see* Armbruster
*International Messenger, see Vsemirnïy vestnik*
*Historiya tsartvovaniya Petra, see* Ustryalov
Italy / Italian, 139, 146n, 153, 158
Ivan V (brother of and coruler with Peter I), 110n
Ivanov, Avtonom, 145

## J

Janizaries / Janizeries / Russ. Yanïcharï, 134
Jesus I the Great / Adyam Sagad I, emperor of Abyssinia, 129, 130–1, 132, 160, 162, 166
Jidda, 133, 138
Joachim (jester of Peter I), 146
John I, emperor of Abyssinia, 128, 129

Johnson, Samuel, 160; *Rasselas*, 122–3 & n, 160, 164
Jones, A. H. M.: *History of Abyssinia, A*, 164
Jonson (son of a Livonian architect), 147 & n
*Journal, see* Dangeau; Peter I: *Zhurnal*
*Journal asiatique*, 162
*Journal de la Régence, see* Buvat
*Journal de Paris, see* Marais
*Journal of . . . Residence in Abyssinia, see* Gobat
Julian Calendar, 109n
Jyasu I, *see* Jesus I

# K

Kalailikoz, Pasha, 138
Kammerer, Albert, 120, 160, 165; *La Mer Rouge, l'Abyssinie, etc.*, 164
Karlowitz Treaty, 136n–37
Kassala, 121
Kazan / Kazan', 146n, 154
Kazdugli, Mustafa Kiaya, 134
Kiev, 143
Korb, Johann Georg: *Diary of an Austrian . . . at the Court of Czar Peter the Great*, 164–5
Korovin, Stepan, 149
Krestos, Haouâryâ, 162; *see also* Christos
Kronstadt, 156
*Kubla Khan, see* Coleridge
Küchelbecker, Wilhelm von, *see* Kyuhel'beker
Kuprulu, Hussein, 137 & n
Kyuhel'beker / Küchelbecker, Vil'gel'm Karlovich / Wilhelm, 123n

# L

La Fère, 139, 149; Ecole d'Artillerie, 149

Lagan', *see* Lahann
Lagona / Lagon / Lahon, *see* Lahona
Lagona Region (equatorial Africa), 156
Lahaina, 124–5
Lahaina (Hawaii), 124n
Laham River, *see* Mai
Lahama, 124n
Lahann (Abram Gannibal's sister), 110 & n, 119, 125–7, 134, 160
Lahen (Abyssinian general), 127
Lahia Dengel, 127
Lahona / Lagona / Lagon, 118–19, 124, 125
Lahontan, Baron Louis Armand de Lom d'Arce de: *Voyage du baron de Lahontan dans l'Amérique septentrionale*, 151
Lalibala, emperor of Abyssinia, 152
Laon, 149
Law, John, 150
Layahan, 127
Leclercq, Henri: *Histoire de la Régence*, 165
Lefebvre, Théophile, 120–1, 124n; *Voyage en Abyssinie*, 165
Le Grand, Joachim, 133, 134; *Voyage historique*, 123, 124, 165
Leningradskaya Publichnaya Biblioteka (PB), *see* St. Petersburg: Publichnaya Biblioteka (PB)
Leninskaya Biblioteka (MB), *see* Moscow: Publichnaya Biblioteka (MB)
Lenita / Lenta, 143–4
Lénore, Countess de D., 150; *see also* P., WORKS: "Arap Petra Velikogo"
Lepanto, 138
Le Perthus, 153

Lestocq, Count Jean Armand de, 146 & n–47 & n
Lestok, Ivan / Hermann, *see* Lestocq
Leutholf, *see* Ludolf
Livonia, 113, 147n
Lobo, Jeronimo, 123, 124, 165
Logo, 119, 120, 122, 123–4, 125, 128, 158–9
Logon-Chuan, 158
Logote / Legote, 120–1, 122, 125, 159
Louis XIV, king of France, 132, 134, 161
Louis XV, king of France, 110n, 148, 150
Louis (French translator), 123n
Ludolf, Job, 120; *Historia aethiopica*, 165
Lutheran, 154

# M

Macalle, 124
Macaulay, James, 123
MacDonnell, Count Charles, 165
Mai Belessan, *see* Belessa River
Mai Laham / Laam, 124
Maillet (French consul), 133, 134
Makarov, Aleksey Vasilievich, 139
Malbazo, *see* "Petrus Aethiops"
Malebranche, Nicolas de, 151
Mantz, P., 163
Marais, Mathieu: *Journal de Paris*, 165
Mareb River, 119, 120, 121, 122, 124, 128, 157
Massawa / Masuah Island, 130n, 131, 132, 133
Masuah, *see* Massawa
Mathew, David: *Ethiopia*, 165
Mauro, Fra, 120
Mecca, 133, 141n
Mecklenburg-Schwerin,

Charles Leopold, Duke of, 110n
Mediterranean, 135
Melakotawit, queen of Abyssinia, 129
*Mémoire historique sur l'ambassade de France à Constantinople, see* Bonnac
*Mémoires d'Afrique, see* Baratieri
*Mémoires de la Régence, see* Piossens
*Memoirs of My Life, see* Grech: *Zapiski*
*Mer Rouge, l'Abyssinie et l'Arabie, La, see* Kammerer
Merville, Michel Guyot de, 150
Mesrah Island, 130
*Messenger of Europe*, see *Vestnik Evropī*
Metz, 139, 149, 153; Ecole d'Artillerie, 149–50
*Metz, see* Poirier
Mihaylovskoe, 109, 113, 116, 155
Minih / Münnich, Count Burkhard Christoph, 110 & n, 154
Modzalevski, B. L., 165
Modzalevski, L. B., 166
Mohammedan, *see* Moslem(s)
Monnet, 160
Monophysites, 128
Monroe, Elizabeth, 164
Montaiglon, A. de, 163
Moscow, 114, 115, 139, 140, 142, 145, 148; Publichnaya Biblioteka (MB), 112
Moslem(s), 117, 118, 127, 128–129, 131, 133, 134, 144, 156, 159
*Moya rodoslovnaya, see* P., WORKS
Mozemleks (in Lahontan), 151
Muhammad Ahmed ibn Ibrahim el Ghazi ("Gran"), 128, 162
Munnai River, 120, 124

Münnich, *see* Minih
Munzinger, Werner: *Vocabulaire de la langue tigré*, 165
Murad ben Magdelun /
"Murat," 132, 133, 134
Mussulman, *see* Moslem(s)
Mustafa II, sultan of Turkey,
133, 137, 138, 141
*My Pedigree, see* P., WORKS:
*Moya rodoslovnaya*

# N

Naples, 139
*Nauka i literatura v Rossii pri
Petre, see* Pekarski
Negro(es), 113 & n, 116–17,
128, 133, 134, 140, 145, 156,
157, 158
Negroid race, 157
New Testament, 152
Nile River, 132, 134
*Northern Bee*, see *Severnaya
pchela*
*Notes pour l'histoire d'Ethiopie*,
see Perruchon

# O

Obel River, 121, 124
Odessa, 107n, 109
Olderogge, D.: *Abissiniya*, 165
Olenin, Aleksey Nikolaevich,
156
Opatovich, S. I., 154, 165
Opochka, 109
Oriental, 126n
Orléans, Philippe, Duke of,
110n, 148, 149, 150
Oromota tribe, 158
Orthodox, *see* Greek Catholic
Osipov, Praskovia Aleksandrovna (b. Vïndomski / Windomsky, m. Vulf), 113n
Ottoman Empire, *see* Turkey

# P

Paris / -ian, 132, 139, 141, 148,
150
Paulitschke, Philippe, 119, 162
PB, *see* St. Petersburg: Publichnaya Biblioteka
Pecherski, Andrey, *see* Melnikov
*Pedigree of My Hero, see* P.,
WORKS: *Rodoslovnaya moego
geroya*
*Pedigree of the Pushkins and
the Gannibals, see* P., WORKS:
*Rodoslovnaya Pushkinïh*
Pekarski, Pyotr Petrovich, 151;
*Nauka i literatura v Rossii pri
Petre Velikom* (Russian
Science and Literature in the
Era of Peter the Great), 166
Perruchon, Jules, 129, 166
Persia, 151
Peter I the Great, tsar, 109 &
n, 110 & n, 112, 115n, 116,
117, 136, 139, 140, 141, 142,
143–8, 149, 152, 153, 154,
156, 164; *Pis'ma i bumagi*
(Letters and Documents),
166; *Zhurnal* (Journal), 166
Peter II, tsar, 110n
Peter III, tsar, 110n
*Peter the Great and the Ottoman
Empire, see* Sumner
Petit, A., 165
Petrov, Pyotr Petrovich (Peter
I's godson), *see* Gannibal,
Abram
Petrovskoe, 113
"Petrus Aethiops" (Pasfa
Sayon Malbazo), 152
Pezhemski, Pyotr, 166
Phoenicia, 127
Piossens, Chevalier de: *Mémoires de la Régence*, 166
*Pis'ma i bumagi, see* Peter I the
Great
Pitts, Joseph, 163

Poirier, Abbé François Jacques, 153; *Metz*, 166

Polotsk, 143

Poncet, Charles, 119–20, 124, 129, 130 & n, 131, 132–4, 158–9, 161, 163; *Relation . . . du voyage*, 166

Popovo, 141

Portugal / Portuguese, 123, 127–8, 130n, 146n, 165

*Portuguese Expedition to Abyssinia, see* Whiteway

*Predki Pushkina, see* P., PUSH-KINIANA; *Pushkin's Ancestors*

Preobrazhenskiy Regiment, 151

Prester John, 161

*Prince of Abissinia, The, see* Johnson: *Rasselas*

Protestant, 128

Pskov / Pskovan, 109, 126n, 155

Pushka, Grigoriy (ancestor of the Pushkins), 111

Pushkin, Aleksandr Petrovich (P.'s great-grandfather), 111

PUSHKIN, ALEKSANDR SERGEEVICH

    LETTER TO: Osipov, P., 113n; WORKS: "Arap Petra Veliko-go" ("The Blackamoor of Peter the Great"), 113–4, 116, 141, 150, 155, 158; *Moya rodoslovnaya* (My Pedigree), 155–6; *Rodoslovnaya moego geroya* (Pedigree of My Hero), 117; *Rodoslovnaya Pushkiníh i Ganibalov* (Pedigree of the Pushkins and the Gannibals), 113, 117; "Table Talk," 145–6; PUSHKINIANA: *In Pushkin's Hand (Rukoyu Pushkina*, ed. Tsyavlovski, L. Lodzalevski, & Zenger), 166; *Pushkin* (Annenkov), 114; *Pushkin and His Contemporaries (Pushkin i ego sovremenniki*), 163, 164; *Pushkin*

*in Moscow (Pushkin v Moskve*, Vinogradov, Chulkov, & Rozanov), 167; *Pushkin's Ancestors (Predki Pushkina*, Vegner), 167; *Works* (1906–15, ed. Vengerov), 165 (1937–50, 1959, ed. Blagoy, Bondi, *et al.*), 166

Pushkin, Aleksey Fyodorovich, 111

Pushkin, Elizaveta (Lev Sergeevich's wife), 157

Pushkin, Fyodor Petrovich, 111

Pushkin, Konstantin (Grigoriy Pushka's son), 111

Pushkin, Lev Aleksandrovich (P.'s grandfather), 111

Pushkin, Lev Sergeevich (P.'s brother), 109, 157

Pushkin, Maria Alekseevna (m. Osip Gannibal), *see* Gannibal, Maria

Pushkin, Nadezhda (Osip Gannibal's daughter, Sergey Pushkin's wife, P.'s mother), 111, 157

Pushkin, Pyotr (descendant of Konstantin, ancestor of P.'s parents), 111

Pushkin, Sergey Lvovich (P.'s father), 111, 112

Pyatnitski Church, 144

*Pyotr I, see* Bogoslovski

Pyrénées-Orientales, 153

# Q

Quartin-Dillon, R., 165

# R

Racine, Jean, 151

Ragusa, 140, 141, 142, 143

Raguzinski, *see* Vladislavich-Raguzinski

Rami Pasha, 138

Rasselas, 123, 160, 161; *see also* Johnson: *Rasselas*
Red Sea, 121, 130n, 131, 132, 133, 135
*Red Sea and Adjacent Countries*, *see* Foster
*Régence galante, La, see* Hervez
*Relation abrégée du voyage . . . en Ethiopie, see* Poncet
Revel / Tallin, 112, 113, 146
*Revue rétrospective*, 165
*Revue sémitique*, 166
Rezanov, Gavrila, 149
Rimbaud, Arthur, 132
*Rimbaud in Abyssinia, see* Starkie
*Rodoslovnaya moego geroya, see* P., WORKS
*Rodoslovnaya Pushkinīh i Ganibalov, see* P., WORKS
Roman Catholicism, 128
Rome / Roman, 117, 118, 123, 127, 153
Rozanov, N. P., 167
*Rukoyu Pushkina, see* P., PUSHKINIANA: *In Pushkin's Hand*
Rumyantsov Museum, *see* Moscow: Publichnaya Biblioteka
*Russian Ancientry, see Russkaya starina*
*Russian Archives, see Russkiy arhiv*
*Russian Biographical Dictionary, see Russkiy biograficheskiy slovar'*
*Russian Gazette, see Russkie vedomosti*
*Russian Science and Literature in the Era of Peter the Great, see* Pekarski: *Nauka*
*Russische Günstlinge, see* Helbig
*Russkaya starina* (Russian Ancientry), 154, 164, 165
*Russkie vedomosti* (Russian Gazette), 162

*Russkiy arhiv* (Russian Archives), 165
*Russkiy biograficheskiy slovar'* (Russian Biographical Dictionary), 166

## S

Saad, Grand Sherif, 133
*Sacred City of the Ethiopians, The, see* Bent
Sagad I, Malak, emperor of Abyssinia, 152
Sagad III, *see* Susneyos
Saillant, Marquis de, 150
St. Basil Order, 143
St. Petersburg / Petersburg / Russ. Sankt Peterburg / Petrograd / Leningrad, 109, 110, 141, 143, 146, 147 & n, 154, 155; Publichnaya Biblioteka / Imperatorskaya Publichnaya / Leningradskaya / imeni Saltïkova-Schedrina (PB), 151
Saint-Simon, Louis de Rouveroy, Duke de, 163
Saint-Yves, Georges, 119, 120
Salt, Henry, 119, 120, 121–2, 123, 124, 125, 131, 140, 164; *Voyage to Abyssinia*, 167
Sanuto, Livio, 120
Scandinavia, 113
Scarperia, *see* Angiolo
Schefer, Charles, 163
Scherer, Johann Benedikt / Jean Benoit, 147n; *Anecdotes*, 146n–47
Schöberg / Scheberch, Christina Regine (m. Abram Gannibal), *see* Gannibal, Christina
Schöberg / Scheberch, Matthias, 154
Schoonebeeck, Adriaan, 148
Selenginsk, 154
Seraoe / Serae, *see* Serawe
Serawe, 120, 124

Serawe Mts., 133
Serbia, 141
Seremai River, 121, 122
*Severnaya pchela* (Northern Bee, ed. Bulgarin & Grech), 156
Shangalla, 128
Sheba, Queen of, 157
Shepelyov, Dmitri Andreevich, 115 & n
Shmurlo, E. F., 146, 167
Siberia / Russ. Sibir', 110, 153
Sinai, Mt., Monastery, 133
Siré, 161
Slavic, 157
*Slovar' dostopamyatnïh lyudey Russkoy zemli, see* Bantïsh-Kamenski
Snitterfield, 160
Solomon, King, 157
Somali, 128
*Some Records of Ethiopia, see* Beckingham
*Sommaire d'un cours d'architecture militaire, see* Belidor
Soulié, E., 163
Soviet, 139
*Sovremennik* (The Contemporary, first ed. P.), 166
Spain / Spanish, 149, 153
Spanish America, 156
Stambul / Russ. Tsargrad, *see* Constantinople
Starkie, Enid, 132; *Rimbaud in Abyssinia*, 167
Stratford on Avon, 160
Suakin, 133
Sudan, 121
Suez, 133, 135
Suida, 155
Sumner, B. H., 142; *Peter the Great and the Ottoman Empire*, 167
Susneyos / Sagad III, emperor of Abyssinia, 123, 128
Sveaborg / Suomenlinna, 123n
Sweden / Swedish, 143
Syria, 135

**T**

"Table Talk," *see* P., WORKS
Tabor, Mt., 161
Tekla-Haymonot I, emperor of Abyssinia, 129, 130, 160
Tellez, Balthazar, 120
Theophanus / Russ. Feofan, 143
Theophilus / Tewoflos, emperor of Abyssinia, 130
Thevenot, Melchisedec, 120
Tigré, 119–20, 124, 127, 129, 130 & n, 131, 132, 135, 152, 158, 159, 161
Tigré-Endorta, *see* Endorta
Tobolsk, 154
Tokule, Mt., 120, 121
Tolstoy, Count Ivan Andreevich, 142
Tolstoy, Count Pyotr Andreevich, 115, 137, 138–9, 142
*Travels, see* Bruce
Tserana, 121
Tsyavlovski-Zenger, Tatiana, 166
Turaev, B. A.: *Abissinskie hroniki* (Aybssinian Chronicles), 167
Turkey / Turkish, 115, 116, 117, 118, 125, 126n, 128, 129, 132, 133, 134–9, 141–2, 144, 147, 148, 152, 158
Tyurikov (court jester), 147

**U**

Ukraintsev, Emelian Ignatievich, 136–7 & n, 141
United States Army Map Service, 121, 124, 125, 167
Ustryalov, Nikolay Gerasimovich: *Istoriya tsarstvovaniya Petra Velikogo* (History of the Reign of Peter the Great), 167
Uvarov, Count Sergey Semyonovich, 156

*Index*

## V

Valentia, George, Viscount: *Voyages and Travels*, 167
Vauban, Sébastien Le Prestre, Marquis de, 149, 153
Vegner, M., 129, 146, 163; *see also* P., PUSHKINIANA: *Pushkin's Ancestors*
Vengerov, S. A., *see* P., PUSHKINIANA: *Works*
Venice, 136n, 143
Versailles, 160
*Vestnik Evropï* (Messenger of Europe, first ed. Kachenovski), 145
*Vicar of Wakefield, The, see* Goldsmith
Vidal, 160
Vignaud, Henri, 165
Vilno, 109, 143
Vinogradov, L. A., 167; *see also* P., PUSHKINIANA: *Pushkin in Moscow*
Vinogradov, V. V., 157
Vladislavich, Luka, 141
Vladislavich-Raguzinski, Count Savva Lukich, 139–43, 148, 154
*Vocabulaire de la langue tigré, see* Munzinger
Voltaire, *see* Arouet
*Voyage du baron de Lahontan, Le, see* Lahontan
*Voyage en Abyssinie, see* Lefebvre

*Voyage historique d'Abissinie, see* Le Grand
*Voyage to Abyssinia, see* Salt
*Voyages and Travels, see* Valentia
*Voyages . . . d'une princesse babylonienne, see* Arouet
*Vsemirnïy vestnik* (international Messenger), 163
Vsesoyuznaya Biblioteka imeni Lenina, *see* Moscow: Publichnaya Biblioteka
Vulf, Aleksey Nikolaevich: *Dnevnik* (Diary), 116, 164, 167
Vulf, Praskovia (b. Vïndomski), *see* Osipov, Praskovia
Vyazemski, Prince Pyotr Andreevich, 156

## W

Warsaw, 143
Wensinck, A. J., 163
Whiteway, R. S.: *Portuguese Expedition to Abyssinia, The*, 163, 167

## Z

Za-Ouald, 159, 161, 162
*Zapiski moey zhizni, see* Grech
Zenger, T. G., *see* Tsyavlovski-Zenger, T.